Encryption for Organizations and Individuals

Basics of Contemporary and Quantum Cryptography

Robert Ciesla

Apress®

Encryption for Organizations and Individuals: Basics of Contemporary and Quantum Cryptography

Robert Ciesla
HELSINKI, Finland

ISBN-13 (pbk): 978-1-4842-6055-5   ISBN-13 (electronic): 978-1-4842-6056-2
https://doi.org/10.1007/978-1-4842-6056-2

Managing Director, Apress Media LLC: Welmoed Spahr
Acquisitions Editor: Celestin Suresh John
Development Editor: Rita Fernando
Coordinating Editor: Divya Modi

Cover designed by eStudioCalamar

Cover image designed by Pixabay

Author photo © 2018 by A.C.

Distributed to the book trade worldwide by Springer Science Business Media New York, 233 Spring Street, 6th Floor, New York, NY 10013. Phone 1-800-SPRINGER, fax (201) 348-4505, e-mail orders-ny@springer-sbm.com, or visit www.springeronline.com. Apress Media, LLC is a California LLC and the sole member (owner) is Springer Science + Business Media Finance Inc (SSBM Finance Inc). SSBM Finance Inc is a **Delaware** corporation.

For information on translations, please e-mail booktranslations@springernature.com; for reprint, paperback, or audio rights, please e-mail bookpermissions@springernature.com.

Apress titles may be purchased in bulk for academic, corporate, or promotional use. eBook versions and licenses are also available for most titles. For more information, reference our Print and eBook Bulk Sales web page at http://www.apress.com/bulk-sales.

Any source code or other supplementary material referenced by the author in this book is available to readers on GitHub via the book's product page, located at www.apress.com/978-1-4842-6055-5. For more detailed information, please visit http://www.apress.com/source-code.

Printed on acid-free paper

Dedicated to curious laypeople everywhere.

Table of Contents

TABLE OF CONTENTS

About the Author

Robert Ciesla is a freelance writer from Helsinki, Finland. He has worked on many video games on several platforms. He is the author of *Game Development with Ren'Py* (2019) and *Mostly Codeless Game Development* (2017). Ever since finishing *A Brief History of Time* by Stephen Hawking in middle school, Robert has been fascinated by the world of quantum mechanics. Robert's bachelor's thesis in journalism took on some questions on how to popularize the core concepts of quantum physics and related fields. He has devoured most relevant books in the field since and continues to explore this area of reality.

About the Technical Reviewers

Paul Love is the Chief Information Security and Privacy Officer at a financial services organization and has been in the information security field for almost 30 years. He has held information security positions at many major organizations including Federal Home Loan Mortgage Corporation (Freddie Mac), Ernst & Young, Microsoft, Schlumberger, Ally Financial, and Fifth Third Bank. Paul started his information security career when he joined the United States Marine Corps, where he served for eight years, eventually achieving the rank of Sergeant.

Paul holds a Master of Science in Network Security, has authored/co-authored nine books on Information Security and Unix/Linux, and has been the technical editor of ten books on Linux and Unix. Paul holds multiple information security and privacy certifications, including Certified Information Systems Security Professional (CISSP), Certified Information System Auditor (CISA), and Certified Information Security Privacy Manager (CISM); multiple privacy certifications including Certified Information Privacy Professional/United States/Europe/Canada (CIPP/US, CIPP/E, CIPP/C); as well as other technical and professional certifications.

Sai Matam is a software architect with over 20 years of diverse experience in software. He has a Bachelor of Engineering from Osmania University. His interests include low latency, highly scalable systems, algorithms, Java, cloud, and Go programming language.

Astha Keshariya, PhD, MSC (Honors), MBA, has consulted and contributed to several commercial and academic organizations in the field of applied cryptography and information security for over 16 years.

Introduction

Cryptography may or may not sound like the sexiest of topics. However, it's essential to nearly everyone plugged into the planetwide community of the Internet. Whether you're working for Area 52 with a Top Secret clearance or shopping online for some swanky items, many elements of cryptography will be present. They not only take the form of virtually unbreakable databases but also (barely noticeable) digital certificates, passwords, PIN codes, and secured email.

As impressive as current-day cryptography is in its security and computational effectiveness, what's behind the corner is even more so. Quantum computing is well on its way. We can expect our world to be profoundly impacted by this paradigm on several levels.

Ultimately, encryption and secrecy are not new phenomena. They have been with us since the earliest days of recorded history, only in more primitive ways. The continuing need for concealing information tells us something about the world at large. I hope this book offers you an understanding of just how big of a deal cryptography actually is.

Encryption for Organizations and Individuals is for the curious layperson. Equations are therefore kept to a minimum. This book is roughly divided into two parts: first, we explore contemporary cryptography, and then we probe into its quantum sibling. I hope my book equips you with the tools you need to take on the quantum computing revolution with some confidence.

CHAPTER 1

The First Era of Digital Encryption

You're probably used to entering passwords into devices by now; it's a part of everyday life, like locking and unlocking one's front door. From email services to mobile devices, we all guard our privacy to a varying extent in the digital realm. And that's exactly how it should be. In this chapter, we'll take a quick look at modern-era digital encryption. But first, we'll revisit some of the most game-changing moments in the historical context of all things cryptographic, as you may not be familiar with the incredibly long history of the science.

Classical Cryptography

Let's first define our main term. The word *cryptography* refers to the science of transmitting messages which remain undecipherable to often malicious third parties. It comes from the ancient Greek words of *kryptos*, which stands for hidden, and *graphein*, which means "to write." Cryptography is valued by warring tribes, governments, and individuals alike; as long as there remains the need for any kind of political action or activism, cryptography will continue to thrive.

© Robert Ciesla 2020
R. Ciesla, *Encryption for Organizations and Individuals*,
https://doi.org/10.1007/978-1-4842-6056-2_1

There are two other terms of relevance you should become familiar with at this point: *plaintext* and *ciphertext*. The former refers simply to an unencrypted message (e.g., "Hello! Apress is the best publisher!"), while the latter covers encrypted messages, which appear nonsensical to those not in possession of the decryption key(s).

Now, the first recorded instance of hidden messages dates back to ancient Egypt, 1900 BC. A series of nonstandard hieroglyphs (i.e., characters in the Egyptian writing system) were discovered carved into the walls of a tomb. Experts still argue whether these messages contain any pertinent information or not; they may have been created with the intention to amuse or confuse.

Clay tablets from Mesopotamia (its area corresponding with most of modern Iraq, Kuwait, and some parts of Syria) indicate attempts at concealing more "serious" information around 1500 BC. Many of the tablets were found to be encrypted cooking notes. These are clearly important state secrets and should never fall in the wrong hands: empires have been known to collapse for less!

The mighty Romans of ancient times, too, were known to utilize cryptography, creating a device called *Caesar's cipher*. It simply involves shifting the alphabet to a degree as agreed upon by two parties (e.g., using a right shift of two letters so that A becomes C and C becomes E). Although hardly representing the state of the art in encryption in 2020, many a private communique was dispatched between Julius Caesar (100 BC–44 BC) and his allies using this technique. It didn't hurt, of course, that most of his enemies were illiterate.

In medieval times, the state of the art in cryptography was to be found among the Arab people. A grammarian from Basra, Iraq, *Al-Khalil (717– 786 AD)*, wrote a seminal work on hidden messages, entitled *The Book of Cryptographic Messages*. His book is famous for its use of permutations and combinations to list all possible Arabic words with and without vowels.

Al-Khalil's work inspired another monumental book in the field, *The Manuscript for the Deciphering of Cryptographic Messages* written by one *Al-Kindi (801–873 AD)*, a mathematician and astronomer from Kufa, Iraq. His work, released around the year 800, detailed most likely for the first time ever the concept of *frequency analysis*, which is still an important concept in cryptography. We will learn more of the basics of Al-Kindi's work in the next section.

The Basics of Frequency Analysis

Frequency analysis is the study of letters contained in an encrypted message in order to reveal at least parts of the plaintext message. The rest should be subject to common sense and basic grammar. Now, most languages have certain letters appearing at a specific frequency. For example, in the English language, the most common letters are E, T, and A. In contrast, Q, X, and Z are not found in English sentences very often. In a historical context, the inventor of Morse code, *Samuel Morse (1791– 1872)*, did his part to discover which letters of the alphabet are the most common in English in order to assign to them the most simple codes.

Let's assume we are to decrypt a message which, we're told, only contains a short English sentence. Knowing this, we may statistically determine some parts of the message and deduce the rest, if we're lucky. The first step is count the times a letter appears in an encrypted message. Now, take a look at the ciphertext we are to decrypt:

KZ GZK ZKGR KKR

Which is the most frequent letter in the example? That would be K with five occurrences. The most common letter was E, right? Changing the K's to E's results in the following:

EZ GZE ZEGR EER

Not much help you may think. However, let's keep at it. The second most frequent letter here is Z with three occurrences. As for the English language, the second used letter is T. Let's go with that.

ET GTE TEGR EER

The third most frequent letters here are G and R, both with two occurrences of each. As for the English language, the third used letter is usually A, I, N, O, or S. Let's go with S first and replace the message's G's with it.

ET STE TESR EER

Our intuition speaks: that can't be right. After careful consideration (and possibly trying all other statistically significant choices of O, N, and I, which got us nowhere), we decided to replace the G's with A's instead.

ET ATE TEAR EER

Now we see something vaguely resembling English. Let's use our incredible powers of deduction and take a wild guess. What if R equals L?

ET ATE TEAL EEL

Finally, some proper English. Oh, those pesky extraterrestrials and their hunger for our majestic (and, let's face it, delicious) Anguilliformes! This has been a simple demonstration of frequency analysis. Using a combination of statistical evaluation and grammatical sense, especially with intelligence concerning the message's language issued beforehand, one may be able to decrypt some of the simpler ciphertexts, all on paper.

Mind you, we could've also deciphered the message even more easily using Caesar's cipher mentioned earlier in the chapter. By switching the alphabet six times to the right (i.e., A equals G, C equals I), we would've achieved the same result.

It should be noted that an Egyptian mathematician *Al-Qalqashundi (1355–1418)* first described the *polyalphabetic system* which greatly undermined the effectiveness of classical frequency analysis. The polyalphabetic system refers to the method of using multiple letters/ symbols per alphabet in a plaintext message to cause further confusion during the decryption process.

The Wonders of Steganography

Steganography is the technique of hiding a message or image within another message or image. Again, the word steganography comes from Greek, consisting of *steganos*, meaning concealed, and *graphe*, meaning writing. Although the term was first used by Johannes Trithemius (1462– 1516), an early German cryptographer and Benedictine Abbot, it's very likely steganography has been around for much longer. Written in 1499, Trithemius' seminal three-volume work *Steganographia* was released much later in 1606. While on the surface it seemed to deal with magic and spirits, it was possibly written to conceal and demonstrate the use of cryptographic methods. Scholars still hold differing views on the matter.

Interestingly, British philosopher and statesman Francis Bacon (1561– 1626) developed a robust steganographic system all the way back in 1605; it's known as the *Baconian cipher*. This consists of hiding messages not via the content of text, but through its presentation (i.e., typefaces). Bacon visually detailed his steganographic method in his monumental 1623 philosophical work *De Augmentis Scientiarum*.

In practice, classical steganography consists of methods such as invisible ink and the correct interpretation of typefaces to deliver messages to those aware of such content. Modern methods include hiding messages in image files and practically any type of file; digital devices and formats lend themselves well to these techniques. One could utilize audio and video as well in this context. Digital steganography took off in the mid-1980s and won't be an abandoned practice anytime soon. State secrets and classified military intelligence will continue to be distributed using this method for the unforeseeable future.

European Developments in Cryptography

Europe, too, made great contributions to the science of cryptography. *Leon Battista Alberti (1404–1472)* was an Italian architect and author who devised a cryptographic tool of his own, known as the *Alberti disk*. The device uses polyalphabetics, as originally introduced by Al-Qalqashandi, in the form of two connected disks each divided into 24 cells. The disk was impossible to break without knowing its inner workings. At the time, it was a revolutionary piece of applied cryptography.

Professor Auguste Kerckhoffs (1835–1903) from the Netherlands published two articles in 1883 that are considered classics in the field. His work entitled "Military Cryptography" was featured in the *Journal of Military Science* in France. Kerckhoffs's articles detailed six principles of practical cipher design, which are still quite relevant today. They are as follows:

1.   The system should be, if not theoretically unbreakable, unbreakable in practice.

2.   The design of a system should not require secrecy, and compromise of the system should not inconvenience the correspondents.

3.   The key should be memorable without notes and should be easily changeable.

4.   The cryptograms should be transmittable by telegraph.

5. The apparatus or documents should be portable
    and operable by a single person.

6. The system should be easy, neither requiring
    knowledge of a long list of rules nor involving
    mental strain.

Principle number 2 is of particular relevance; it's also referred to
as *Kerckhoffs's law* or *Kerckhoffs's axiom*. It states that a cryptosystem
should never be vulnerable even if all facets about said system, apart
from the decryption key, are public. Although still popular among some
government agencies, *security by obscurity (STO)* is mostly an obsolete
approach among cryptographers of today. Obscurity shouldn't be
considered a factor at all when designing secure systems. If government
civil servants defect, for example, your system eventually becomes
compromised. STO provides, at best, a layer of pseudo-security.

Some of Kerckhoffs's principles are no longer valid, as computers
have become advanced enough to handle complex calculations in mere
milliseconds. Also, not many people use telegraphs as of 2020 (although a
company called iTelegram has been founded).

At the End of Classical Cryptography

The era and techniques described in the previous sections form a concept
called *classical cryptography*. As you probably noticed, it was mostly based
on various aspects of linguistics and physical/visual methods. The type of
information classical cryptography has an effect on is limited. But we're
now moving on to the modern era of all things cryptographic. This is where
it gets somewhat complicated – and exciting.

The Digital Cryptographic Revolution

Like many other areas of modern life, computers revolutionized cryptography. In fact, they offered unforeseen possibilities that offered completely secure messaging, a feat almost impossible using traditional methods. Eventually, cryptography was combined with the cutting edge of sciences, including quantum physics. But we're not going there yet; let's have a review of what got us there first.

In 1943 during World War II, British cryptography experts (sometimes called "codebreakers") created the first programmable digital computer, the *Colossus*. It was primarily devised to intercept German military intelligence, but it also helped usher in a new era in electronics. Its German counterpart was the *Lorenz cipher*, a fearsome piece of machinery with a near-perfect track record of encrypting intelligence. However, due to human error, the Lorenz cipher's way of operating was ultimately figured out by the British without ever actually getting their hands on one. Colossus itself was a state secret up until the mid-1970s, with many of the units having been destroyed in the previous decade by the British government.

Strangely, it was only in the 1970s when academia started taking cryptography seriously en masse. Corporations soon picked up the trend; IBM was among the first major companies to develop cryptographic systems and techniques. Their work had a big impact on the US government's data protection policies, for one.

Digital Encryption 101

Encryption in the digital realm consists of basically three things: *an encryption method, an encryption key*, and a *decryption key*. An encryption method is the mathematical means of how a message or file is scrambled to appear completely random to a third party. Only the party with a decryption key (i.e., a password) can access the plaintext contents of the file.

Now, there are two widely used encryption approaches in the world today (not to be confused with encryption algorithms, which are a separate concept): *symmetric* and *asymmetric (i.e., public-key cryptography)*. The former uses a single key for both encryption and decryption of the data. The latter uses two separate keys: one public and one private. With this asymmetric approach, the public key is used to encrypt data, while the private key is used for decryption. In a classic example, *Bob* uses *Alice's* public key to encrypt some data. Upon receiving it, *Alice* then uses her private key to decrypt the contents.

Under most circumstances, it's impossible to discover the private key using the public key. Symmetric cryptography is known to be speedier if dealing with large quantities of data. However, the asymmetric approach provides additional security.

Now, a bit is the smallest unit of measurement in data sciences, being represented by either one or zero. The strength of an encryption standard is usually apparent in the amount of bits it carries. There are encryption standards ranging from 40 to 256 bits and more. A couple of these will be discussed next with more elaboration on them coming up later in the book.

The Diffie–Hellman Key Exchange

One of the earliest public-key encryption protocols was the Diffie–Hellman, named after cryptologists *Whitfield Diffie* and *Martin Hellman*. This protocol allows for two parties without any prior knowledge of one another to create a shared secret key/password. The process is done over an insecure channel. Once the shared key is formed, any communications can be secured with it in a separate encryption method. The Diffie–Hellman approach was published in 1976.

Let's go through a simplified Diffie–Hellman exchange. In real-life situations, the numbers would have to be much larger to provide an acceptable degree of security. First, Alice and Bob decide on a modulus (p) and the base (g). Usually the modulus (p) is a large prime number, while the base (g) is kept small to keep things simple.

We'll pick **19** for the modulus and **6** for the base. Next Alice and Bob choose their secret numbers. Let's say Alice (a) picks **5** and Bob (b) picks **2**. The capital A represents the result Alice will send to Bob. Note: *Modulo* is simply the operation of finding the remainder after division of a number by another one.

a = 5 (Alice's choice)

A = ga mod p

= 65 mod 19 = 5

b = 2 (Bob's choice)

B = gb mod p

= 62 mod 19 = 17

Now we calculate Alice's and Bob's secret keys in public without a care in the world:

secretkeya = B a mod p = 175 mod 19 = **6**

secretkeyb = A B mod p = 52 mod 19 = **6**

If both secret keys turn out identical, and they do, the key exchange has been successful. The shared secret number in our example turns out to be 6, which is also the base number. This is not always the case. Rather it's due to us using such small numbers in our example.

The Data Encryption Standard (DES)

The fruit of the interest of IBM in cryptography turned out to be the *Data Encryption Standard (DES)*. This is a flawed but influential encryption symmetric method/algorithm. Released in 1977, the standard initially provided adequate encryption of data and protection against cryptographic attacks, such as *brute-force attacks* which consist of a system/actor trying to enter every single password possible. However, as of 1998, DES was compromised within three days using a computer network created by the *Electronic Frontier Foundation (EFF)*. As of late, due to the increase in computing power, systems encrypted using DES can be compromised within 23 hours. Therefore, the standard is obsolete. You may have noticed an option in some older routers/modems, for example, to secure your wireless Internet connection using DES. Please do not.

DES, despite all the brouhaha back in the day, was only 56-bit long. So it offers 72,057,594,037,927,936 (i.e., 2^{56}) permutations of passwords, which is also known as *key space*. By today's standards, that's not impressive. Any 128-bit (2^{128}) encryption method, on the other hand, provides a key space of 300,000,000,000,000,000,000,000,000,000,000,000,000 (or 300 decillion) permutations. Now we're talking.

There were corrective measures applied on DES, however. In 1984, a standard called *DESX* was introduced by MIT Professor *Ron Rivest*. His standard added two auxiliary keys to the single 56-bit one found in the original DES, each 64-bit wide. In theory this results in a key space of 184 bits; in practice it's somewhere between 88 and 119 bits. DESX never really took off.

In 1995, an algorithm called *Triple DES* (also stylized as *3DES*) was released. It consists of three rounds of encryption applied to each data block, hence its name. Despite a theoretical key space of 168 bits, which sounds rather impressive, the standard has an effective key space of 112 bits. While better than the original algorithm, Triple DES is still subpar and best avoided. Also, the method is quite slow compared to some of the newer algorithms. Microsoft, for one, did wisely write off Triple DES from its Office 365 platform in 2019. Unfortunately, it does remain in use in some electronic payment services, including the smart payment card varieties of *Visa* and *Mastercard* as of 2020.

In Closing

After reading this chapter, you should have an understanding on the history of cryptography and how it relates to current-day electronics. You absorbed information on the following:

- A concise history of cryptography

- Elementary frequency analysis

- The beginning stages of digital cryptography

- The basics of current-day encryption technologies

In the next chapter, we'll begin to explore the world of digital encryption in full force. In particular, you'll learn about the venerated RSA algorithm.

CHAPTER 2

A Medium-Length History of Digital Cryptography

Having taken a look at the basics of digital cryptography in the previous chapter, we'll now move on to some specifics of the topic. We'll take a gander at technology, which is both historically significant and still relevant in the field today. We'll also cover some important related standards organizations and unlock several concepts crucial in the world of cryptography.

RSA: The First Big Public-Key Cryptosystem

In the previous chapter, we discussed the first federally approved symmetric cryptosystem, the *Data Encryption Standard (DES)* of 1977. You probably also remember the concept of public key (i.e., asymmetric) cryptosystems from said chapter. We'll now discuss perhaps the greatest asymmetric system of them all: the mighty *RSA*.

© Robert Ciesla 2020
R. Ciesla, *Encryption for Organizations and Individuals*,
https://doi.org/10.1007/978-1-4842-6056-2_2

Now, the RSA algorithm was first presented to the public in 1978 and it consisted of all the factors public-key cryptosystems of today possess. RSA stands for *Rivest–Shamir–Adleman*, based on the three inventors behind it. The trio went on to win the prized *ACM Turing Award* for computer science in 2002. The other two scientists, *Ron Rivest* and *Adi Shamir*, have enjoyed long and successful careers in fields such as cryptography and mathematics. Since 2000, RSA has been classified as patent-free. The algorithm is used in several Internet-related technologies, including TLS (transport data security) (i.e., online URLs that begin with *https://*) and PGP-based email encryption.

The RSA algorithm derives a pair of keys based on two large prime numbers. One of these keys represents the public key, while the other is kept private. One cannot derive the private key from the public key. However, if the two originally used prime numbers are known to a malicious actor, the private key can be computed, hence making the encryption unsafe.

As for prime numbers, they are natural numbers greater than ones (1) that can't be generated by the multiplication of two smaller natural numbers. The following are all prime numbers: 5, 7, 17, and 23. The following are not: 4, 8, and 10. As with many things in mathematics, there are an infinite number of prime numbers out there in the universe(s). As of 2019, the largest known prime number is 24,862,048 digits long. Yes, that's only the amount of digits, not the number itself. Note: Nonprime numbers (e.g., 4, 8, 10) are referred to as *composite numbers*.

Relatively prime numbers (i.e., *coprimes*) also exist; these are groups of numbers that have a greatest common divisor of 1. For example, 3 and 4 are a duo of relatively prime numbers, but 2 and 4 aren't. Coprimes are actually a big deal in RSA as you will learn next.

Generating Keys in RSA

The following are the main phases in RSA key generation for both the public and private keys. Many algorithms have similar approaches to that of RSA on a theoretical level. However, for the purposes of this book, we'll examine RSA's inner workings only to a degree. You don't have to understand much of the following to utilize encryption in your personal or professional life, but it might come in handy.

1. First, two preferably large prime numbers are chosen at random and similar size in their number of bits. Ours won't be that large for the sake of simplicity. These prime numbers are usually labeled p and q. Let's say p = 5 and q = 17.

2. p and q are then multiplied and stored in variable **n** *(n=pq)*. **n** is one half of the public key. In our example, n = 85. *n* should also be of the chosen bit length, for example, 1024 bits in size with p and q at 512 bits in length. Small sizes, that is, 256 bits or less, aren't considered secure enough. Again, our simple example will overlook this requirement.

3. Next, we summon the so-called Euler's phi function (symbolized with ϕ):

    $\phi(n)=(p-1) * (q-1)$ or in the case of our chosen numbers: $(5-1) * (17-1) = 64$

4. To calculate the public key, we will choose a value for a new variable **k**, so that k and $\phi(n)$ from the previous phase don't share any factors besides 1. Popular choices for k include the prime numbers 17, 257, and 65537; let's pick the biggest number of the bunch. We can denote this function in the following

manner: $gcd(k, \phi(n))$ or in the case of our example $gcd(65537, 64)$. gcd stands for *greatest common divisor* and it's used to check for coprimes. Again, if we get a result of 1 (and we do), all is well. Now *(n, k)* is your full public key.

5. To generate the private key we'll be storing in a variable named *d*, we execute the *extended Euclidean algorithm* like this: $d=(1/k)mod\phi$. Note: 1/k is a modular multiplicative inverse of d, not a literal division.

The greatest common divisor is best derived using the *basic Euclidean algorithm*. This method refers to the factorizing of the two numbers in question and the multiplication of their common factors.

Here's another example of the basic Euclidean algorithm as in how to count the greatest common divisor. Let's have some jolly good fun with two composite numbers. The number 64 can be factored like this: 2 x 2 x 2 x 2 x 2 x 2. The other number we'll pick, 1096, can be factored like so: 2 x 2 x 2 x 137. These numbers have three common factors (2 x 2 x 2). We can discard the rest. Therefore, the gcd for this pair is 8, which is denoted as follows:

$gcd(64, 1096) = 8$.

Encrypting and Decrypting in RSA

Let's say *Alice* gives her public key (consisting of variables *n* and *e* as per the previous section) to *Bob*, who is eager to send a message, denoted by variable *m*, back to Alice. First, Bob inserts a touch of gibberish into *m* by running it through a *padding scheme*. This is standard practice in RSA to confuse any potential attackers (which we will tackle later in the book). Then, he creates the encrypted message *c* (referring to ciphertext) by calculating the following: $c=m^e \bmod n$.

Now, having just received c from our friend Bob, and wanting to transform it into plaintext m, Alice will compute the following sequence: $m-c^d \bmod n$. Alice simply utilized her private key consisting of variables d and n to achieve this. The decrypted message will be padded as per the padding scheme implemented prior to encryption, so it needs to be unpadded before plaintext m is usable.

In Through the Trapdoor

Another important addition to your cryptographic vocabulary is the concept of *trapdoors*. These refer to mathematical functions that are easy to compute in forward direction, but impossible to reverse; in our context we're usually dealing with factorization problems. Trapdoor functions were coined and introduced in the 1970s by mathematicians *Diffie*, *Hellman*, and *Merkle*. They are a core component of many public-key cryptosystems, including the RSA algorithm.

The Strengths and Weaknesses of RSA

As previously mentioned, the use of RSA is extremely widespread with the majority of Internet-related security certificates (i.e., those signed with RSA keys). Standardized for online use in 1994, RSA is a mature technology with plenty of research behind it; any design flaws in the system have been addressed a while ago.

However, the *RSA Problem* has been formulated; this refers to the possibility of decrypting RSA ciphertexts using only the public key. For encrypted data with key sizes of 1024 bits or more, no solution to the problem exists as of 2020: such data is quite safe. However, datasets encrypted with lower key sizes may turn out to be vulnerable. RSA relies on *random number generators (RNGs)* in its key/password generation. RNGs in the context of RSA are programs that create prime numbers that are supposedly impossible to guess at a later stage. This is not the case, at least not 100% of the time, and has proven to be a security issue for RSA, too.

Not many varieties of RNGs are in use and some predictability in them has been discovered. Two groups of researchers from Europe and the United States made a startling discovery in 2012: some 27,000 public RSA keys offered no security. The researchers used several databases of these keys, including those found at *Michigan Institute of Technology (MIT)* as well as those provided by the *Electronic Frontier Foundation (EFF)*. They examined a total of 7.1 million public keys. However, it's safe to say RSA is still a safe cryptosystem at least over 99% of the time; it hasn't been anywhere near fully compromised. There are no practical reasons to abandon it anytime soon.

Some of the issues with RSA's security are actually found in the hardware sector. A select few manufacturers of Internet-related hardware, like routers and game consoles, seem to prefer flawed RNG software in their products due to cost-related reasons. These devices are supposed to provide encrypted wireless connections and/or other forms of security, so they, too, rely on random number generators, which may or may not be always up to the task.

Also, although very robust in security, RSA is a relatively slow method for encryption of larger datasets. In fact, it's often used simply to encrypt passwords used in faster, symmetric algorithms such as the *Advanced Encryption Standard (AES)* described in Chapter 3. For this purpose, at least even RSA is perfectly suited for in 2020 and beyond. This approach is sometimes referred to as *hybrid cryptography*.

The ElGamal Cryptosystem

Continuing our historical cryptographic review, we're now moving onto *Miami Vice*, large haircuts, and padded shoulders; we're in the 1980s. Egyptian cryptographer *Taher Elgamal* presented his own take on public-key cryptosystems in 1985. The system was a success and is still used in many modern security software suites, like the *GNU Privacy Guard* and *Pretty Good Privacy (PGP)*. These two suites and more will be discussed in depth later in the book.

The ElGamal encryption method is based on the difficulty of discovering a *discrete logarithm* in a cyclic group. A cyclic group (G) is a set created from a single element, containing element *g* and a single *associative binary operator*. All elements in these types of groups can be obtained by applying the group's binary operation to *g* or its inverse. The ElGamal cryptosystem is partially based on the *Diffie–Hoffman key exchange method (DH)* which was explained in Chapter 1.

Like RSA, ElGamal is somewhat slow in its operation and is often used to encrypt the keys/passwords of symmetric cryptosystems, which usually work faster. ElGamal is therefore often used in tandem with modern symmetric algorithms like the *Advanced Encryption Standard (AES)*.

Digital Certificates

Certificates are basically messages with the public key and identity of some entity. This message is digitally signed by some other entity, such as a certificate authority. Because the message is signed, it remains unalterable. This very property ties a public key to an identity. Proper authentication of the owner of a public key is of paramount importance. Literally anyone can generate public keys and publish them under any name they desire. Without proper measures, an impersonator can access encrypted messages meant to be served to any individual. Digital certificates and public-key infrastructures, introduced in the next section, were created to address this issue.

Public-Key Infrastructure (PKI) and Certificate Authorities (CA)

An important security measure in asymmetrical encryption is called *public-key infrastructure*. This refers to the practice of having specific policies and procedures for the management of digital certificates and public keys.

In a PKI system, public keys are tied to specific entities (i.e., individuals and businesses). This process is done by an actor known as a *certificate authority (CA)*. As mentioned before in this chapter, the most common use of PKI is found in an online environment in the form of SSL/TLS certification (i.e., the technology which secures websites).

So, a CA simply issues certificates that contain the public key and the owner's identity. An appropriate private key isn't publicly available, but instead kept hidden by the user who created the pair of keys in the first place. In general, digital certificates are valid for a few years at a time. Certificate authorities' public keys are often hard-coded into operating systems or browsers to make tampering with them very difficult. Upon receiving one of these digital certificates, we can be quite sure they are authentic.

Most CAs are operating on a purely national level, due to local laws affecting these procedures. An exception to this is *Let's Encrypt*, a nonprofit certificate authority created in 2014 by the *Electronic Frontier Foundation*, *Mozilla* (creators of the Firefox browser), *University of Michigan*, *Akamai Technologies*, and *Cisco Systems*. Unlike most certificates issued, these are only valid for 90 days. As of 2018, the top three certificate authorities were *IdenTrust*, *Comodo*, and *DigiCert*. Out of these, IdenTrust has worked with Let's Encrypt to cross-sign their intermediate certificates so that Let's Encrypt certificates would function in all major browsers.

Web of Trust (WOT)

An alternative to the PKI system is known as the *web of trust*. In a cryptographic context, this refers to a system devised in 1992 by *Phil Zimmerman*, the creator of the original *Pretty Good Privacy (PGP)*. Trust translates to binding an identity to a public key. If one obtains public key of A with a signed message from A, binding another public key and identity of B, then we can assume the new public key belongs to B.

Instead of using certificate authorities, a web of trust system operates on the level of *identity certificates* issued by individuals themselves. For one, having a certificate system remain independent from any companies guarantees immunity against bankruptcies. Also, being decentralized, WOT is a technology which avoids the possibility of a single point of failure present in many PKI systems.

More on SSL/TLS

As mentioned, perhaps the most commonly encountered use of certificates is to be found in the online realm of the SSL/TLS protocol. SSL stands for *Secure Sockets Layer* and remains a popular way of encrypting data online; TLS refers to *Transport Layer Security* and is simply a newer and improved version of the same technology. A website secured with SSL/TLS will result in an encrypted connection that is very hard to eavesdrop on. You're visiting a secure website if its address begins with *https* instead of *http*.

On an algorithmic level, SSL/TLS can utilize one of several popular encryption methods, including RSA and the DSA, as described next. As of 2020, you should stick to TLS as SSL is a deprecated standard.

FIPS and Digital Signature Algorithm (DSA)

Federal Information Processing Standards (FIPS) are public information processing standards created by the *National Institute of Standards and Technology (NIST)*, for use in computer-based systems of nonmilitary US government agencies. They encompass cryptographical algorithms and related methods.

A popular FIPS-compliant method for encrypting signatures, the *Digital Signature Algorithm*, emerged in 1994. DSA is currently fairly widely used as a part of some SSL/TLS-based solutions in place of the RSA encryption method. Although patented, DSA is available for worldwide implementation royalty-free. Like the RSA, DSA uses a key pair consisting of a public key and a private key. The latter is used to create digital signatures for messages, which in turn can be verified using the signer's reciprocal public key.

Have Some Standards for Goodness' Sake

There are a number of prominent standards organizations that are very much involved in current-day cryptography. We'll take a quick look at some of them next; you should be roughly aware of what they do and how they relate to the world of computer science and cryptography.

First, we have the *Telecommunication Standardization Sector (ITU-T)* of Switzerland that has its roots in the *International Telegraph Union (ITU)* founded all the way back in 1865. The format behind TLS/SSL and many other public-key certificates is known as the *X.509 standard*, which was created by ITU-T in 1988.

The *National Institute of Standards and Technology (NIST)* is a nonregulatory agency of the *US Department of Commerce*. Since its inception in 1901, NIST's mission has been to promote innovation and industrial competitiveness. The organization's *Cryptographic Technology (CT) Group* has worked extensively on cryptographic technologies over the years.

In 2013 NIST was accused of providing backdoors (i.e., methods of decrypting encrypted data outside of using the normally required keys) in their encryption standard *SP800-90* for the exclusive use of the *National Security Agency (NSA)*. They responded by stating NIST is required to work with the NSA by statute and they also do benefit from NSA's expertise in the cryptographic field. Nonetheless, an updated standard, *SP800-90A*, was made public in 2015, ostensibly without any backdoors.

American National Standards Institute (ANSI) is a nonprofit and private organization that inspects standards for products and technologies mostly in a US-based context. ANSI also facilitates the use of American engineering in Europe and elsewhere in the world. As of 2020, the organization is an adorable spring chicken at 102 years old. While ANSI doesn't develop standards per se, it oversees the development and use of standards by other parties. Important standards designated by the organization include *ANSI C*, a standardized version of the C programming language, and the now obsolete *Data Encryption Standard (DES)* as discussed in the previous chapter.

Next, the *International Organization for Standardization (ISO)* was founded in 1947 in Geneva, Switzerland. The organization promotes worldwide proprietary, industrial, and commercial standards. The ISO holds general consultative status with the *United Nations Economic and Social Council,* which in turn aims to "conduct cutting-edge analysis, agree on global norms and advocate for progress." One of ISO's most relevant publications in the cryptographic field is the *ISO/IEC 18033-1:2015*, which is a multipart international standard specifying most of current state-of-the-art encryption systems.

Finally, we have the *Institute of Electrical and Electronics Engineers (IEEE)* which is an association for electronic and electrical engineering professionals founded in 1963. With its 420,000 members, the IEEE yields major influence in all things engineering; the association aims to better the education and technology in the field. The IEEE produces over 30% of the world's literature in computer science, including cryptography, in the form of over 100 peer-reviewed journals.

In Closing

By finishing this chapter, you hopefully have gained some knowledge on how popular cryptosystems operate on a theoretical level. You absorbed information on the following:

- How prime numbers are used in the context of cryptography

- What the RSA algorithm is and how it operates on a theoretical level

- RSA's main strengths and weaknesses

- What *public-key infrastructure (PKI)* means

- What *certificate authorities (CA)* and *web of trust (WOT)* refer to

- A primer on some of the most well-established standardization organizations

The next chapter will focus on the de facto universal encryption standard: the incredible *Advanced Encryption Standard (AES)*. This algorithm is at this very moment protecting most of our encrypted devices and systems.

CHAPTER 3

The AES and Other Established Cryptographic Technologies

By now, you're aware of some historically relevant cryptographic concepts and how prime numbers relate to encryption algorithms. In this chapter we're moving on to the current-day de facto cryptographic staple, the Advanced Encryption Standard (AES), in addition to tackling many other relevant concepts in the field. We will first visit some basics, including the two major numeric systems in computer science: binary and hexadecimal, for those who feel they need a refresher.

Variables and Arrays 101

Since AES incorporates matrices (i.e., multidimensional arrays), we'll start with the related basics. You can skip this section if it sounds familiar.

First, a *variable* is an arbitrarily named piece of data which holds information. That may be a letter (e.g., "B"), a single word, or a very complex number. *Arrays* are a different kind of data type. They are

© Robert Ciesla 2020
R. Ciesla, *Encryption for Organizations and Individuals*,
https://doi.org/10.1007/978-1-4842-6056-2_3

collections of the aforementioned variables with each included variable being indexed for easy access. See the following example written in the C programming language; fear not, we won't be dwelling deep into programming anywhere in this book! A very crucial concept to digital encryption, prime numbers, was introduced in the previous chapter. Let's name our variable accordingly.

```
int prime_numbers = { 941, 373, 311, 83 };
printf(" Ryker's favorite number is %d", prime_numbers[2],"!" );
```

First, we created an array called *prime_numbers* to host four integers, that is, numbers which can only be written whole, as in *373* and not *373.5*. Then we accessed and displayed the third variable in this array, that is, *311*, using index position 2. In the context of computer science, array indexing usually starts at 0 (e.g., 0, 1, 2, …), and not 1 (e.g., 1, 2, 3, …) like us humans might expect.

Binary and Hexadecimal

We should now take a quick gander at the two of the most relevant numeral systems in computer science and, naturally, in cryptography as well. It's quite important to know how to interpret a value in any of the numerical systems mentioned in this section. If your math is sort of rusty, do read on and master the information; otherwise, you can skip this section.

All of us are familiar with the *decimal system*, sometimes also called the *base-ten system*. Decimal digits range between 0 and 9. This is a people's system as computers prefer other types of numerals, as you will learn next.

Binary represents a numerical system with only two symbols: 0 and 1. Also known as the *base-two system*, binary is what digital devices use to function on the most basic level.

Note   In some types of binary operations, you will be often equating 1 for *true* and 0 for *false*.

The third important numerical system is known as *hexadecimal, base-sixteen*, or simply *hex*. In addition to the decimal range of 0 to 9, this system also uses the letters A to F to represent values between 10 and 16, that is, 11 in the decimal system is represented by the letter B in hex. This means the hexadecimal system has a total of 16 different symbols for representing values. Hex bodes well to high informational density: with only two digits, we can summon numbers up to 255. In binary, we would need eight digits.

Converting Decimal to Binary

We'll start with decimal to binary conversion. Let's take the decimal value of, say, 86, and transport it into the magical realm of binary notation. The end result is 1010110. And how, you may ask? Well, think of it this way: binary numbers are collections of flags with only two positions – on and off. Binary notation starts at 1 and advance to the left with each value having twice that of the one to its right.

In our example, we start with the "flag" at number 64 (see Table 3-1). Does 64 go into 86? Oh yes. What about 32? No, then it's too big. 16? Yes. We are now at 80. We just have to find the remaining 6 and we do that by setting the flags at 4 and 2 to "heck yes" and we're done. We have thus demonstrated that 86 in decimal is indubitably 1010110 in binary. We may denote it as follows: $(86)_{10} = (1010110)_2$

Table 3-1. *A simple demonstration of converting the decimal number 86 to binary*

Decimal value	64	32	16	8	4	2	1
Binary value	1	0	1	0	1	1	0

For another example, 13 in decimal would be, you guessed it, 1101 in binary, that is:

$$(13)_{10} = (1101)_2$$

Note   There are two concepts you might come across which should be addressed at this point: the *most significant bit (MSB)* and the *least significant bit (LSB)*. The former refers to the first bit (i.e., the leftmost) in a binary string as it yields the largest value. The latter, which is found at the last digit in a binary string, only holds the value of one (1) at most.

Converting Decimal to Hexadecimal

To honor our planet's oceanic life, let's take the number of currently discovered crustacean species (e.g., crabs, lobsters, and shrimp), which happens to be **67,000**, and convert that into hexadecimal, shall we? We'll start by dividing said number with 16, and keep doing this until the result of this division reaches zero. The remainder from each division is then marked in hexadecimal notation; after each division, anything after the decimal point is to be discarded. The number of steps it takes to reach the end result dictates the number of digits we need. Finally, the row of remainders (in hex) is reversed and you've completed the conversion (see Table 3-2).

Table 3-2. *The conversion process of the number 67000 in decimal to hexadecimal*

Step #	Operation	Result	Remainder in Decimal	Remainder in Hex
1	67,000 ÷ 16	4187	8	8
2	4,187 ÷ 16	261	11	B
3	261 ÷ 16	16	5	5
4	16 ÷ 16	1	0	0
5	16 ÷ 1	0	1	1

As for the result, the hexadecimal value we were after is **105B8**. We may denote it as follows: $(67000)_{10} = (105B8)_{16}$

Converting Binary to Hexadecimal (and Vice Versa)

The conversion process of binary to hex (or vice versa) is a relatively simple one. Let's first tackle the conversion from binary to hexadecimal. We'll start by mapping out all 16 symbols of the hexadecimal system in binary (see Table 3-3). Now each symbol in hex has a corresponding four-digit symbol in binary (and it's always four digits in this context).

Keeping up with our oceanic theme, let's take the number of species of eel (i.e., 800) and rearrange it from binary to hexadecimal. First, we need to find what 800 is in binary. That happens to be **1100100000** (see the segment entitled "Converting Decimal to Binary" previously in this chapter). Now, we simply divide that binary value into groups of four digits and refer to Table 3-3 for the corresponding hex symbol. We get three groups: 0011, 0010, and 0000. This means the desired result is **320**. In other words, $(1100100000)_2 = (320)_{16}$

Table 3-3. *All 16 hexadecimal symbols and their binary counterparts*

Binary	Hex	Binary	Hex
0000	0	1000	8
0001	1	1001	9
0010	2	1010	A
0011	3	1011	B
0100	4	1100	C
0101	5	1101	D
0110	· 6	1110	E
0111	7	1111	F

As for the reverse? Take the hexadecimal value of, say, **CACA**, which also happens to be the name of a somewhat obscure Goddess in ancient Roman mythology (look it up). Now, the only thing we need to do for this type of conversion is to once again ogle at Table 3-3 and pick our corresponding four-digit binary symbols for each hex symbol. So, **CACA** in hex is **1100 1010 1100 1010** in binary. Simple, isn't it?

Classifying Bits

Unless you're familiar with the many units used in digital information, you should take a peek at Table 3-4; it lists some terms which will be visited and revisited many a time later in this book and in the world of cryptography as well.

Table 3-4. *Some common units of digital information*

Digital Unit	Number of Bits
Bit	1
Nibble	4
Byte/octet	8
Word	16
Double word	32
Quad word	64
Kilobyte (KB)	8192
Megabyte (MB)	8388608

The Indomitable AES

By the early 1990s, the Digital Encryption Standard (DES) from 1976 was rapidly becoming obsolete. The 56-bit keys/passwords simply weren't secure enough due to increases in computing power. Even the much more robust Triple DES algorithm (mentioned in the previous chapter) wasn't a good enough successor as it lacked speed even in purely hardware-based settings. According to a guidance paper published by the National Institute of Standards and Technology (NIST) in 2018, 3DES is being retired. These guidelines propose that 3DES is deprecated for all new applications and it's completely gone after 2023 (Barker & Roginsky, 2019).

Now, an open selection process for a successor to DES, the AES algorithm, was held by the NIST in 1997. This approach garnered support from the cryptographic community as it negated many backdoor-related issues. A total of 15 submissions were made, including algorithms called *MARS* (devised by IBM), *CRYPTON*, and *Rijndael*. Created by two Belgian cryptographers, *Vincent Rijmen* and *Joan Daemen*, the Rijndael method took first prize. The NIST picked up and renamed Rijndael to publish the *Advanced Encryption Standard (AES)* in 2001. Approved by the US Secretary of Commerce, AES became an official federal government standard in May of 2002. Like its predecessor the DES, AES is a symmetric encryption system, meaning there is only one key/password used for both encryption and decryption of data.

Note   For perspective, using technology available in 2020, it would take approximately one billion billion years to break even the weakest form of AES encryption (i.e., the 128-bit variety). It's best not to try and/or to think about it.[1]

Implementations of AES

The AES system is provided free of charge for any purpose, private or commercial; the standard is not only made available for the US federal government. Numerous popular software products utilize AES. These include file compression tools *7-Zip*, *Roshal Archive (RAR)*, and *WinZip*. We'll go in depth into the vast world of AES-based software in the next chapter. Also, processor giants *Intel*, and as of late *AMD*, include hardware-based AES acceleration in many of their CPUs making cryptographic operations faster than ever on their newer platforms. This hardware-based acceleration technology is known as *AES New Instructions (AES-NI)*. Under ideal settings, AES-NI can make your cryptographic operations ten times faster.

---

[1]M. Arora: "How Secure is AES against brute force attacks?", EE Times, 2012

Block Sizes and Key Lengths

Getting into the technical side of things, we'll begin with *blocks*. In the context of cryptography, these refer to an often fixed-sized amount of data which is to be operated on by an algorithm at one time. The AES, for example, processes data in 128 bit blocks only (which is the same as 16 bytes). Encrypted files use as many blocks that are needed to include all of the plaintext/unencrypted data. If a plaintext fails to fill the last block, the remainder is filled with the so-called padding (i.e., random data in most cases) using a *padding scheme*, which we briefly touched upon in previous chapter. We'll examine this concept in depth later in this chapter, too.

Now, just to reiterate: *key length* refers to the number of bits available to a key/password in a specific cryptographic system (see Table 3-5). A theoretical 2-bit key length would offer a whopping two different key alternatives.

The now-obsolete DES offers a 56-bit key length, providing an initially impressive 7.2×10^{16} combinations. The strongest form of AES, as in its 256-bit variety, gives us a hefty 1.1×10^{77} key combinations, which, again, is very hard to break (Oppitz & Tomsu, 2018).

Table 3-5. *Some popular bit widths and their associated possible number of keys*

Bit Width	Possible Number of Keys
128 bits	$2^{128} = 340{,}282{,}366{,}920{,}938{,}463{,}463{,}374{,}607{,}431{,}768{,}211{,}456$
192 bits	$2^{192} = 6{,}277{,}101{,}735{,}386{,}680{,}763{,}835{,}789{,}423{,}207{,}666{,}416{,}10$ $2{,}355{,}444{,}464{,}034{,}512{,}896$
256 bits	$2^{256} = 115{,}792{,}089{,}237{,}316{,}195{,}423{,}570{,}985{,}008{,}687{,}907{,}853{,}$ $269{,}984{,}665{,}640{,}564{,}\ 039{,}457{,}584{,}007{,}913{,}129{,}\ 639{,}936$

The Substitution–Permutation Network (SPN)

The most prominent feature in AES is a concept known as the *substitution–permutation network*. An SPN performs several rounds of processing on a dataset for encryption. These rounds consist of both substitution and permutation of data with the creation of the so-called round keys for each round. These are temporary keys created by the algorithm to "unlock" the next round. *Substitution* simply means replacing a symbol with another. *Permutation* refers to the rearrangement of the values already present in a dataset.

The more of these obfuscation rounds is used, the harder the data in question is to be compromised. In AES, the key size determines the SPN rounds to be used (see Table 3-6). For critical data it's important to always choose the largest key length AES has to offer (i.e., 256 bits).

Table 3-6.   *The AES key lengths and how they relate to the SPN rounds*

Key Length	SPN Rounds	Block Size
128 bits	10	128 bits
192 bits	12	128 bits
256 bits	14	128 bits

Row- and Column-Major Orders

AES operates on a 4 × 4 **column-major order array** which is referred to as a *state*. This *state* consists of blocks which are 16 bytes in size each. *Row-major order* and *column-major order* are methods for storing two-dimensional arrays in linear storage such as hard drives or random access memory (RAM).

See Figure 3-1 for an illustration on how row-major and column-major orders differ in their approach. In the context of AES, only the latter is relevant; the figure also demonstrates what an "AES state" looks like (i.e., a four by four matrix of data).

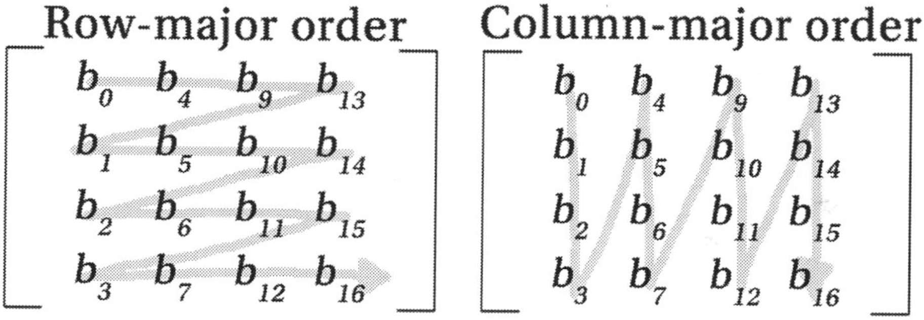

Row-major order   Column-major order

$$\begin{bmatrix} b_0 & b_4 & b_9 & b_{13} \\ b_1 & b_5 & b_{10} & b_{14} \\ b_2 & b_6 & b_{11} & b_{15} \\ b_3 & b_7 & b_{12} & b_{16} \end{bmatrix} \qquad \begin{bmatrix} b_0 & b_4 & b_9 & b_{13} \\ b_1 & b_5 & b_{10} & b_{14} \\ b_2 & b_6 & b_{11} & b_{15} \\ b_3 & b_7 & b_{12} & b_{16} \end{bmatrix}$$

Figure 3-1. *Row-major and column-major orders. The latter is relevant in AES*

Note   A row-major order is sometimes referred to as the *lexographical access order*, and column-major orders can be called by the fancy term of *colexographical access orders*.

The Steps in an AES Encryption Round

Whereas the older DES algorithm was bit-based, AES operates with bytes (i.e., groups of eight bits). AES operates largely in a so-called Galois field. This is a mathematical space where there are a limited number of integers (i.e., values) in the field. At the core of the AES algorithm are four major stages with some of them divided into subphases. They are first listed in this section and then discussed further.

1. **Key Expansion**. Takes place once. The round keys are generated using an algorithm called the *key schedule*.

2. **Initial Round Key Addition**. Takes place once. Each byte in the "state" (i.e., the AES matrix) is combined with a block of the round key.

3. **A Stage with Four Steps**. Takes place 9, 11, or 13 times.

   1. **SubBytes**. A step where each byte in the state is replaced with another according to a lookup table.

   2. **ShiftRows**. The last three rows of the state are shifted cyclically by a specific number of steps.

   3. **MixColumns**. An operation which combines the four bytes in each column.

   4. **Add Round Key**

4. **Last Round.** Takes place once.

   1. SubBytes

   2. ShiftRows

   3. Add Round Key

Remember, in AES the key length determines how many rounds the algorithm repeats. Next, we'll go through each of these steps in greater detail.

Key Expansion

In the first step, an algorithm called the *key schedule* is used to create a set of round keys from the original key/password. AES uses a separate 128-bit round key for each round and also creates one additional key.

AES key expansion is divided into the following substeps:

1. A *RotWord operation* performs one-byte left bit shifting on a word, that is, [B0, B1, B2, B3] becomes [B1, B2, B3, B0].

2. *SubWord* is executed for a byte substitution on each byte using the S-box.

3. Finally, the result of steps 1 and 2 has an XOR operation applied on it with an AES round constant, *Rcon*. This constant holds a different value each round.

Initial Round Key Addition

After summoning the key schedule, each byte of the state is merged with a block of the round key. This is done using the *exclusive OR* binary operator (i.e., XOR) on the datasets. The result after this operation is 1 if only the first bit is 1 or only the second bit is 1. The result will be 0 if both are 0 or both are 1 (see Table 3-7). So, if we were to XOR the bit values of, say, 10011 and 11100, the result would be 01100. This operator is often denoted with the symbol ⊕.

Table 3-7. The output from an "exclusive OR" (XOR) operator

Bit Input A	Bit Input B	XOR Result
1	1	0
1	0	1
0	1	1
0	0	0

A Stage with Four Steps

SubBytes

This step involves replacing each of the 16 array elements in the AES state with those from a lookup table, known as the *S-box*, which is short for *substitution-box*. An S-box in AES takes eight bits of information (i.e., one byte), mapping it into this lookup table and producing different eight bits of output data (see Table 3-8). The S-boxes themselves are generated using specific algorithms which are out of the scope of this book.

Now, let's say we have this byte getting fed into the S-box: 0001 0010. This byte will be split in half, creating two 4-bit values (i.e., nibbles). We then convert these values into hex and get the result of 1 and 2, respectively. Now, the first value/nibble (in our case the number 1) is used to find the row placement in the lookup table. Obviously, the second nibble (in our case 2) tells us which column in the S-box AES is looking at. In our example, the substitute number would be 39. Naturally, when the SubBytes routine is executed, it's used on the contents of an entire AES state (i.e., the 4 x 4 matrix of data).

Table 3-8. *A partial AES S-box. Note the use of hexadecimal numbering*

	0	1	2	3	4 ...
0	52	9	6a	d5	30
1	7c	e3	**39**	82	9b
2	54	7b	94	32	a6
3 ...	8	2e	a1	66	28

ShiftRows (And a Primer on Bitwise Shift Operators)

Next, we'll be shifting the 16 byte blocks in the 4 x 4 state grid to the left by specific amounts. In AES the first row isn't manipulated in this step. However, each block in the second row is shifted one place to the left. The third row is offset by two and the fourth row is offset by three places, all to the left. See Figure 3-2 for a visual demonstration of this phase. Naturally, blocks shifted out of the state's left periphery don't disappear; instead, they reappear on its right side.

The AES *"shift rows"* step

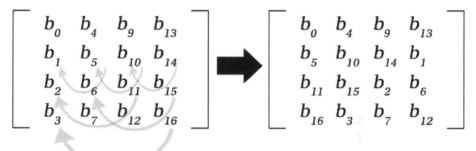

Figure 3-2. *The shift rows step in AES. Notice how the first row isn't altered*

These types of operators are called *bitwise shift operators* in the world of computer science. They are used to shift binary data not only to the left, but also to the right. Time for an example. Note: Left and right bit shifts are often denoted with << and >>, respectively.

```
0010 << 2 → 1000
0010 >> 1 → 0001
```

The binary string 0010 in decimal represents the number two (2). In the first example, we performed a bitwise shift to the left by two bits, resulting in the binary string of 1000. Converted into decimal, that would result in the number eight (8). So, for one, a single bit shift left doubles a variable's value.

Next, we performed a single bitwise shift right on the same binary string of 0010. This resulted in 0001, which is the number one in both binary and decimal. Bitwise operators are universally used not only in cryptography, but in virtually all programming situations due to their effectiveness; they tend to be easy on the CPU and not eat a lot of resources.

MixColumns

All of the columns of four bytes are next transformed by the means of matrix multiplication. This function takes as input the four bytes of one column and outputs four completely new bytes, which replace the original column. The result is another new AES state consisting of 16 new bytes. This step is not performed during the last round.

Add Round Key

In this step the previously generated subkey (i.e., round key) is merged with the current state. The subkey is added by combining each byte of the state with the corresponding byte of the subkey using the bitwise operator XOR.

The Last Round

This round consists of one more execution of the aforementioned steps of SubBytes, ShiftRows, and Add Round Key; MixColumns is not applied at this stage. And now your plaintext is rather securely encrypted, especially if you chose to use ASE's 256-bit key length with its 14 rounds of operation. However, there is a trade-off concerning the speed of the decryption with these longer key lengths.

Decryption in AES

Reaching the plaintext in a dataset encrypted in AES is relatively simple: most of the preceding steps are reversed. However, the same S-box used during the SubBytes phases during encryption cannot be used for decryption; the said lookup table needs to have an inverted counterpart at that point.

Now, here are the steps for decrypting in AES:

1. **Key Expansion**

2. **Add Round Key**

3. **Reverse ShiftRows**

4. **Reverse SubBytes**

The following four steps are repeated 9, 11, or 13 times (for 128/192/256 bits, respectively):

1. **Add Round Key**

2. **Reverse MixColumns**

3. **Reverse ShiftRows**

4. **Reverse SubBytes**

And finally, a single **Add Round Key**-step is executed..

Hash Values: Digital Fingerprints and Checksums

Hash values, as briefly mentioned in the previous chapter, are ways of identifying messages. These values offer robust and secure identification. We'll now examine the concept of hashing in more detail.

First, be aware that hashing isn't the same as encryption. A hash value is more like a unique digital fingerprint for a file. In most cases they're almost impossible to reverse engineer and can thus be used for secure identification of datasets. Simply put, a hashing algorithm creates a fixed-sized value (i.e., a value that is always the same bit width, no matter of the input) out of variable-sized data (e.g., collections of images, text files, or audio files). The output of a hashing algorithm is sometimes called the *message digest*.

For example, the text string of ***Apress is a great publisher!*** becomes the following (MD5 algorithm) hash value: **0503ff3cb7e1c6f28064e63fc 5efa0b1**. The much shorter message of ***Hello!*** results in this hash: **952d2c 56d0485958336747bcdd98590d**. Although the messages are of different sizes, the hash values consist of the same amount of digits, that is, there's 32 of them in these and any others (processed with MD5).

Note   MD5 and other hashing algorithms will be discussed in depth later in the chapter. Also, most hash values, including the ones mentioned earlier, are based in the hexadecimal numeric system.

Collisions

In theory, no two hash values are the same: this is what allows for their exceptional usefulness in digital identification. However, an undesirable scenario in hashing exists where there are in fact two identical values; this is known as a *collision*. Hash values are created using a variety of different algorithms. An ideal hashing algorithm is one which doesn't facilitate any collisions to occur. In reality, some of them do not exactly fit these criteria. Next, we'll take a closer look at some of the most popular algorithms for hashing purposes. For the purposes of this book, we don't need to dwell in the inner workings of hashing algorithms, but you should understand why they're needed.

Message Digest 4 (MD4)

The MD4 hashing algorithm was published by *Ronald Rivest's* RSA Labs in 1990. A compromised hashing algorithm, MD4 is still used in some parts of user authentication in *Microsoft Windows* operating systems, including versions 7, 8, and 10. As of all the way back in 1995, MD4 has been considered pretty much obsolete in cryptography circles; it's no longer considered a true one-way function (Leurent, 2008). Please avoid using this hashing algorithm in your personal or organizational projects altogether.

When it comes to Microsoft products and the vulnerable MD4, the security issues are rarely critical. *Active Directory (AS)* is a Windows-based service for authenticating and authorizing users and devices. A part of AS is called *NT LAN Manager (NTLM)*, which is an older authentication method still using MD4 hashing. NTLM can be swapped for a more robust authentication protocol called *Kerberos* in Windows. NTLM is only there for reasons of backward compatibility. Also, Kerberos is turned on by default in more modern versions of the Windows operating systems.

Message Digest 5 (MD5)

Published by RSA Labs in 1992, the MD5 is still a widely used algorithm for hashing purposes. The fifth version of RSA Labs' technique, MD5, creates 128-bit hash values.

Despite its continuing popularity, the algorithm has weaknesses, most notably demonstrated by the Flamer malware in 2012. This is a piece of malicious software originally created for cyber espionage. In fact, the MD5 is rather notorious among cryptographers due to its proneness for collisions and is best avoided for identification in 2020 and beyond. For data integrity verification (i.e., *checksums*), the MD5 is still very much useful; it can be successfully used to verify a file transferred via, say, the Internet, actually arrived intact. Many Linux-based operating systems, as well as Android, use MD5 checksums.

Secure Hash Algorithm 1 (SHA-1)

The NSA came up with the Secure Hash Algorithm 1 (SHA-1) in 1995. This algorithm produces a 160-bit digest upon its execution, which is quite a bit more than what MD5 is capable of. The SHA-1 is a certified US Federal Information Processing Standard (FIPS). However, the algorithm hasn't been considered fully secure since 2005. SHA-1 fell on even harder times in 2017, when all major web browsers ended their support for the algorithm in their SSL/TLS certificates (these were discussed in the previous chapter). Riddled with collision potential, SHA-1 is best avoided.

Secure Hash Algorithm 2 (SHA-2)

A group effort from NIST and NSA, the Secure Hash Algorithm 2 (SHA-2) was made public in 2001. Instead of a fixed 160 bits, the follow-up to the original Secure Hash Algorithm offers the digest sizes of 224, 256, 384, and 512 bits. That's some serious bit width right there and a great improvement over the original algorithm. All algorithmic varieties of SHA-2 seem to be collision-resistant. Also, the SHA-256 hash algorithm is ubiquitous in the world of cryptocurrency, as it's used by *Bitcoin* and several other virtual currencies.

Secure Hash Algorithm 3 (SHA-3)

The latest in the SHA family of hashing algorithms is the Secure Hash Algorithm 3 (SHA-3), once again created by the NIST. Released in 2015, this algorithm uses a so-called sponge approach in which data is absorbed into a *sponge function* and the result is then "squeezed" out. Again, the inner workings of this algorithm are beyond the scope of this book. SHA-3 is also known as *Keccak*.

However, it is to be noted that although SHA-3 offers the same digest sizes of its predecessor SHA-2, it also has two new variants to its algorithm: *SHAKE128* and *SHAKE256*. While these two operate in 128 bits and 256 bits internally, their message digest length can be arbitrarily chosen. Either one of the SHAKE algorithms could be assigned to produce a hash value of 20, 21, or, say, 60 bits in width.

Padding

The term *padding* in cryptography refers to the adding of gibberish into encrypted data. This often helps to further protect the plaintext messages in encrypted datasets. There are several techniques for padding in the current day. AES, for one, works with many of these varieties. Let's take a quick glance at some of the most popular methods.

Bit padding is used by the previously mentioned hashing algorithms, MD5 and SHA; it involves adding an extra bit and possibly an arbitrary number of zeros (e.g., *1000 00*) to the end of a data block. The *ANSI X9.23 standard* uses a byte-sized approach, outputting random bytes after a packet of data (as a reminder, one byte equals eight bits). *Zero padding* is the elegant, but efficient approach of adding a random number of zeros after data. Again, all padding techniques add to the security of encrypted and/or hashed data.

Would You Like Some Salt with Your Data?

Salting is not a concept only used in food-related spaces. In cryptography, it refers to the augmentation of a key/password with additional randomly generated symbols without the key holder being aware of them (see Table 3-9). This makes for far more robust security than a simple key. Salt strings can be of any length. For our purposes, let's use a small 8-bit (i.e., 4-byte) variety of hexadecimal values.

Table 3-9. *Some salted passwords. Salts can either go in front of or after the key*

Password/ Key	Random Salt Value	Password & Salt	Final Hashed Value (with MD5)
happy	d5530386	*happyd5530386*	edf5631950caaaf4d68662c4394d7c44
sad	6df9b90c	*6df9b90csad*	ee1d2475de02e1285d03e633ec9f4e89

In essence, salting creates relatively safe passwords out of even the easiest ones to guess (e.g., *password* or *12345*). Salted keys are usually fed to hashing algorithms for all the security benefits they endow; they also negate the so-called dictionary attacks which consist of the attacker entering thousands or millions of dictionary words into a prompt. For a real-world example, many email providers use salting as an additional security measure on their services.

Best Salting Practices

Salt strings should be long enough. We used short 8-bit salting in our example (as in 4 bytes, or eight characters), which wouldn't be adequate in some real-world scenarios. In general, the amount of salting should be reflected by the message digest size of a hashing algorithm. For older hashing techniques, such as the 160-bit MD5, 8 bits might've actually been adequate. When it comes to 256-bit hashes or bigger, you could pair those with a larger salt.

Also, salts should be randomly generated and unique, incorporating aspects like date or time. It would be a big mistake to include the same exact salts in a system, but it's known to happen. In addition, a system administrator should keep their salt-generator code (or any parts of it) offline and behind closed doors at all times. And use fierce encryption on the key database.

How About Some Pepper?

Salting isn't the only method of increasing password/key security. A method cleverly called *peppering* exists. For the most part, it's an identical approach to salting with one major difference; in peppering the "peppered" data is kept hidden and not stored in a database. A pepper is usually a static, system-wide value which is never made public for any user; it's hard-coded into software. Due to the aforementioned reason, peppers are safe against database breaches. The static nature of peppers is somewhat problematic as you cannot change them easily, if at all. Should a pepper leak, it would cause major security issues, forcing a complete redesign of the compromised system.

Also, for maximal security benefits, a cryptographer could use both salting and peppering in their password policies.

Stretching Keys

A concept related to salting and peppering, *key stretching* refers to enhancing the protection against brute-force attacks a weak key/password offers by adding to the time it takes to enter/guess a password. This basically works by feeding the original key into an algorithm which adds a considerable amount of additional data into it, resulting in a so-called enhanced key. This is usually a key of 128 bits in width or more. Since the enhanced key is such a large piece of data, it'll take the attacker much more time and resources to discover it, increasing a system's level of security greatly.

Cyclic Redundancy Check (CRC)

Let's explain these three letters which may appear from time to time in your cryptographic adventures. *Cyclic Redundancy Checks* are a type of error checking in the digital realm, much like checksums mentioned earlier in this chapter.

CRC works by the sender of a file injecting extra bits into the data to be sent. This file is then transmitted through a network (e.g., the Internet, local area networks). Next, the results between the sender's and receiver's CRC bits are compared. If they match, the data packets have been received in full. Expressed on a more technical level, data sent through a CRC system gets a check value attached to it, which is based on the *remainder* of a *polynomial division* of their contents. There are about a dozen different varieties of CRC for various scenarios, but for the purposes of this book, a cursory look at this concept will suffice.

As a reminder, a *polynomial* is an expression consisting of one or more variables (often designated with the letter x). The following two expressions are examples of polynomials:

$x^2 - 3x + 2$, $4x^2 + 2x - 8$

Modes of Operation

Before ending this chapter, we will address an important part of cryptographic solutions: *modes of operation*. We will revisit some of these concepts later in the book from the context of the most popular operating systems. These operating modes are not exclusive to AES; they can be applied to any block cipher. Modes of operation are an important part of a group known as cryptographic primitives, which refer to well-established algorithms used as building blocks for secure systems.

Block Ciphers and Stream Ciphers

There are roughly two types of ciphers: block ciphers, as in the AES, and stream ciphers, such as the *Rivest Cipher 4 (RC4)* or *Salsa20*. The latter process data one bit (or byte) at a time instead of as blocks of data. Stream ciphers mix pseudorandom data with the plaintext message. These types of ciphers offer real-time operation, as the complete dataset doesn't have to be transmitted before decryption can occur.

Electronic Code Book (ECB)

A weak method, the electronic code book technique provides an identical encrypted result for each identical block of plaintext data. Often a hefty salting scheme is necessary to make the ECB operating mode usable. It does feature *parallelization*, which refers to simultaneous processing of multiple blocks of data; this can reduce overhead considerably on systems with multiple CPU cores. However, ECB is not a recommended mode of operation under any circumstances.

Cipher Block Chaining (CBC)

In this method each block (apart from the first one which uses a random seed) is processed using data from the previous one. While more robust than ECB, data encrypted using cipher block chaining is more prone to data corruption. It will only take a handful of flawed bits due to, say, a transmission error in a single block to compromise the integrity of the rest of the data. Also, unlike the otherwise inferior ECB mode, CBC is *sequential* (i.e., nonparallelized) during encryption. Despite its potential issues, CBC is the most commonly used operating mode as of 2020.

Counter Mode (CTR)

The counter mode is a fully parallelizable stream cipher. This basically means a block-based cipher (e.g., AES) being used as a stream cipher. CTR offers random access processing during both encryption and decryption, which is beneficial in scenarios such as disk drive encryption. Also, this mode, when implemented properly, can leverage the many varieties of special processing instructions found in most modern CPUs to further boost its operating efficiency (e.g., technologies like *MMX* and *SSE*).

In Closing

After finishing this chapter, you will have hopefully gained awareness of the following:

- What the Advanced Encryption Standard (AES) is and when it's used

- What the binary and hexadecimal systems are and how to convert between them

- How the substitution–permutation network (SPN) in AES works

- What steps are a part of a single round of operation in AES

- What hashing means and what some of the most popular algorithms for this are

- What salting and peppering refer to in the context of cryptography

In the next chapter we'll go deep into the world of encryption software, including methods included in popular operating systems as well as some of the most relevant third-party products.

References

Oppitz, M., Tomsu P. (2018). Inventing the Cloud Century: How Cloudiness Keeps Changing Our Life, Economy and Technology. Springer.

Leurent G. (2008) MD4 is Not One-Way. In: Nyberg K. (eds) Fast Software Encryption. FSE 2008. Lecture Notes in Computer Science, vol 5086. Springer, Berlin, Heidelberg.

Barker E., Roginsky A. (2019). Transitioning the Use of Cryptographic Algorithms and Key Lengths. NIST Special Publication 800-131A, revision 2.

CHAPTER 4

You, Your Organization, and Cryptographic Security

Now that you've got some theoretical know-how on how cryptography works, it's time we apply this on a practical level. In this chapter we'll be examining some popular operating systems and how they handle cryptographic matters. We'll also be looking at other types of related software and how they can help you and your organization in maintaining privacy and any potential trade secrets. Let's start off by defining (and/or revisiting) some concepts relevant to all forms of digital cryptography.

Storage Devices, Sectors, and Blocks

It's indeed time we get practical. In order to get to the gist of how encryption works in the real world, we need to look at the most common ways of storing digital data: hard drives and related storage devices. By now you've seen the ads, bought the computer(s), and owned different hard disks in the process. You've probably heard of 500 Gigabyte drives

© Robert Ciesla 2020
R. Ciesla, *Encryption for Organizations and Individuals*,
https://doi.org/10.1007/978-1-4842-6056-2_4

and 10 Terabyte ones, understanding the latter provides much more room for your music, photos, and software. Let's switch on a dweeby electron microscope and take a good look at how bits are actually organized on a hard drive and a solid-state drive, as it all relates to many facets of digital cryptography.

In the context of hard drives, a *sector* usually refers to a physical piece spanning 512 bytes (i.e., 4096 bits). This was, and to an extent still is, the minimum storage unit on most of these devices. However, newer generation hard drives using a technique known as *Advanced Format (AF)* have their sectors set at 4096 bytes (i.e., 32,768 bits). Now, a concept closely related to a sector is the *block*. These refer to anything between a single sector and groups of sectors (e.g., you may have one block which spans four sectors or one block which includes only one sector). So, a block is an abstraction which represents the smallest unit of storage on a storage device. Blocks are needed because an operating system can't possibly access all sectors on an individual basis: there's simply a limited amount of "handles" or IDs available in an OS for that purpose. Using the block approach allows operating systems to support larger drives.

The next generation of hard disks is the *solid-state drive (SSD)*. Unlike hard disks, these types of drives have no moving parts and are thus faster and more energy-efficient. These storage devices utilize semiconductor cells for their functioning instead of rotating physical disks. The smallest unit of storage in an SSD is called a *page*. This generally refers to 4 kilobytes of data (i.e., 4096 bytes or 32,768 bits). From an operating system's and a user's perspectives, SSDs work the same as hard drives. As with hard drives, an SSD's data space is grouped into blocks by an OS enabling a limited amount of file handles to access all of the drive.

Here's digital media organization in a yellow walnut: a *sector* on a **hard drive** usually refers to its smallest unit of storage spanning either 512 or 4096 bytes. The smallest unit of storage in a **solid-state drive (SSD)** is called a *page*. This usually refers to 4 kilobytes of data (i.e., 4096 bytes). *Blocks* are groups of sectors assigned by an operating system.

The Wonders of File Systems

A *file system* is a piece of software which manages how and where data on a storage device is maintained. Different operating systems may have different, and sometimes incompatible, file systems. Commonly, an operating system has both a proprietary file system format and several more or less universally compatible file systems at its disposal. Let's review some of the most common file systems and how they relate with one and other (see Table 4-1).

Table 4-1. *A summary of current-day file system support between operating systems*

File System	MacOS	Linux	Windows
NTFS	Software required	Software required	Supported
Mac OS Extended (HFS+)	Supported	Configuration required	Software required
Apple File System (APFS)	Supported	Software required	Software required
FAT	Supported	Supported	Supported
exFAT	Supported	Supported	Supported

The **FAT** file system (an abbreviation of *File Allocation Table*) is both old and almost universally supported. Most operating systems can read and write FAT-formatted devices (e.g., hard disks and USB devices) without installing any additional software. This system does have its limitations. For one, an individual file has the upper size limit of 4 gigabytes. As of 2020, FAT is still on occasion used on memory cards among other applications.

In 2006 Microsoft released the **exFAT** file system. It was well received and became the de facto standard on SD memory cards, for one. Gone was the file size limit of FAT; in exFAT, a single file can be up to 128 petabytes in size (i.e., 10^{15}). As of recent years, most operating systems have a robust support for exFAT right out of the box.

The once-ubiquitous **Mac OS Extended (HFS+)** file system is still quite widely in use due to literal decades of development and proliferation. Starting its life in 1998, it was Apple's main file system until 2017 with the introduction of the **Apple File System (APFS)**. Although readable by most modern Windows OSs, disks formatted in either HFS+ or APFS require special software to enable any writing/saving functionality. One notable maker of such tools is *Paragon Software*. They provide Apple-related disk access solutions for both Windows and Linux environments.

Apple OSs utilize *Journaling*, which is a feature that keeps records of any changes to files on a disk. This log is stored as a unique data structure called the *Journal*. This helps a system to recover after abrupt shutdowns due to, say, power outages.

Apple's HFS+ file system can be in most cases used on Linux without special software, but that requires an extra step of configuration before you can reliably both read and write HFS+ data on the Linux side of the fence. So prior to using the disk in Linux, connect said device to your Mac and enter the following command in the Terminal program:

```
$ sudo diskutil disableJournal "/Volumes/diskname"
```

This disables journaling on the disk and you should now have a fully operable drive in Linux. Using devices formatted in Apple's latest file system in most Linux distributions (i.e., AFPS), however, requires dedicated software.

Disabling journaling on a MacOS boot/system hard drive is very risky. Do not do that! Only consider that for nonsystem and/or noncritical hard drives.

Volumes and Partitions

Now, we must tackle two more important concepts: the *volume* and the *partition*. In the context of modern operating systems, a partition is a storage area within a single file system. Basically, partitioning is the act of dividing a storage device into smaller pieces. For example, you could partition a 500 gigabyte hard drive into two partitions, both of which are 250 GB in size. You could also get creative and opt for a, say, single 20 GB partition and a 480 GB one with said hard drive, for whatever purposes. In Windows context, partitions ready for use are assigned drive letters (e.g., C, D, E). After this, they are referred to as *volumes*.

Full-Disk Encryption (FDE)

In many cases it's beneficial to encrypt an entire hard drive or drives. This way an entire dataset is unreachable to most malicious parties. Many, but not all, encryption software suites provide this functionality. While not impenetrable (as we will learn in the next chapter), FDE is a must for mobile devices at the very least. Its only trade-off is a mostly negligible slowdown of a computer as the device needs to constantly work in tandem with the encryption process.

File Containers

One doesn't need to encrypt entire disks; *file containers* are virtual disks of arbitrary size that for an outsider look like single files full of nonsense. Once a file container is created, it can only be accessed using the right kind of software and, naturally, the correct key/password. Pretty much all third-party cryptographic software suites provide the functionality of creating these types of files in case you have a handful of sensitive data (e.g., unflattering mankini or swimsuit photos) you want to conceal from the world at large.

Pre-boot Authentication (PBA)

The boot disk refers to the hard drive which contains a computer's operating system, such as Windows or Linux. *Pre-boot authentication* is a technique which allows one to prevent an operating system from starting (i.e., booting up) unless a password is provided. Naturally, in this context the password is issued by the operator of an encryption tool (i.e., you) and not an OS.

Trusted Platform Module (TPM)

Software alone doesn't always guarantee a secure system, usually only the addition of dedicated hardware creates truly robust security. A *Trusted Platform Module* is an international standard for hardware-based cryptoprocessors, as standardized by the *International Organization for Standardization (ISO)* and *International Electrotechnical Commission (IEC)* in 2009.

Basically, a TPM offers random number generation, secure password generation, and the remote means of a third party to verify that the system hasn't been compromised. Physically, TPMs are usually small chips that connect directly into a computer's motherboard. Their manufacturers include *Intel*, *IBM*, and *Samsung*, to name just three.

Block Cipher Operating Modes

Like you may know by now, the AES algorithm, which we became acquainted with in the previous chapter, is a so-called block cipher. These are systems which crunch data in specific amounts (i.e., blocks) at a time. For AES, this block is 128 bits long. As for the primordial DES algorithm, it's a mere 64 bits at a time. Now, AES and other block ciphers/algorithms can function in a variety of ways. These are known as *operating modes* and they will be briefly discussed next.

Cipher block chaining (CBC) is a mode of operation where the data in one block is used to alter the next block. With CBC, we begin by summoning an arbitrary number, known as the *initialization vector (IV)*. This number is only used once per session. The IV is then hit with an *exclusive OR* bitwise operation (i.e., the mighty XOR as discussed in the previous chapter). The aforementioned initial steps create the first data block in the CBC technique. Next, this value is connected, with another XOR operation, to the second block of data. And so the system continues until all of the data blocks have been processed and chained together.

The block size of the encryption algorithm being used in CBC determines the length of the initialization vector (IV); in the case of AES, that would be 128 bits. Naturally, for DES the IV would only be 64 bits long.

As useful as CBC is, a more robust cipher operating mode called *AES-XTS* was introduced in 2010. This mode uses two AES keys: one for the encryption and the other for a so-called tweak value. The tweak key is to be at least 128 bits in length. Simply put, it strengthens the original AES key; a 256-bit AES key size would become 384-bit wide if used with the AES-XTS method.

This approach guarantees that each data block is filled with different data even when issued with identical input. Also, since in AES-XTS data blocks aren't chained, any corrupted bits in a data block do not "spread" into subsequent ones and merely damage the block they occur in (this is known as the *avalanche effect*). AES-XTS is becoming very popular in flash drives and other portable media devices.

Encryption in Modern Operating Systems

Most popular operating systems have built-in facilities for encryption (see Table 4-2). In general, at least the latest versions of these encryption tools are easy to use and offer a high degree of security. Of course, you may opt to use a third-party encryption solution, just in case you feel uneasy about potential backdoors in these systems.

Table 4-2. *A summary of built-in encryption solutions on modern operating systems*

Operating System	Windows 7, 8, 10	Linux	MacOS
Software	BitLocker	Linux Unified Key Setup (LUKS)	FileVault 2
Algorithm/Key Size	AES 128-/256-bit	Variable	AES-256 bit
Operating Mode	CBC, XTS-AES*	Variable	XTS-AES

*= Windows 10 only

Encryption in MacOS: FileVault and FileVault 2

Apple's popular line of operating systems has a reputation for robust whole disk encryption, at least since the 2011 release of *OS X Lion (10.7)* and with it, *FileVault 2*. Now, the first version of *FileVault* (introduced in *OS X Panther, 10.3*) had the lackluster approach of only encrypting a user's home directory. While this protected most of a user's documents, it still potentially offered malicious actors quite a reach into a computer. In addition, FileVault was somewhat slow in its operation, being based on virtual disk images (called *sparse images* in this context). Finally, in 2006 legacy FileVault was completely compromised by the *Chaos Computer Club (CCC)*, which is the largest association of hackers in Europe. Avoid the first version of Apple's encryption for critical data. Laypeople may still not get into your first-generation FileVault disks, but experts sure can.

With a barely noticeable performance hit, FileVault 2 takes on a vastly improved approach offering full-disk encryption for the first time built-in into MacOS. In addition, FileVault 2 creates a recovery key, an alternate password, which you may either write down and store it securely, or tie it into your Apple account on the *iCloud* online ecosystem. If you choose the former, you only get one look at this key: scribble it down carefully. With its many strengths and few (addressed) issues, as of 2020 FileVault 2 is a good choice for smaller organizations and individuals. As always with proprietary encryption software, a backdoor may be present for the US government to sneak in through.

Turning on **FileVault 2** on MacOS (10.7 or newer) is simple. Click *System Preferences* ➤ *Security & Privacy* ➤ *FileVault*. Click the lock icon on the bottom left and enter your user password. You can now enable disk-wide encryption by clicking *Turn on FileVault*.

Windows and BitLocker

Most recent versions of Microsoft's Windows operating systems ship with a versatile encryption tool called *BitLocker*. In addition to offering a traditional password-based system, users can opt to authenticate themselves on BitLocker using several hardware-based methods, adding combinations of TPM and USB devices into a security solution (see Table 4-3). In theory, the more measures you have implemented, the more secure your system is likely to be.

Table 4-3. *A summary of BitLocker authentication mechanisms*

Password	TPM-device and USB-stick
TPM-device and password	USB-stick only
TPM-device, password, and USB-stick	TPM-device only

In addition to its great feature set, BitLocker supports the implementation of an older Microsoft encryption technology, *Encrypting File System (EFS)*. Like its name states, EFS operates on a file-level using a combination of public key (i.e., asymmetric) cryptography and symmetric key cryptography. Ultimately, EFS is only as strong as the user's Windows password as the two are very much intertwined. Combined with BitLocker, however, this issue is negated making for a very capable duo of security measures. EFS has been available since 2000 with the launch of *Windows 2000*; it's still implemented in several of Microsoft's professional operating systems.

Besides all of its strengths, BitLocker is considered lacking in one aspect: it's closed source. You may or may not choose to believe Microsoft when they stated there are no backdoors in the software. However, unless an organization is in direct opposition to the US government, BitLocker is a fine choice for all your system-wide cryptographic needs. See Table 4-4 for the varieties of Windows shipping with most up-to-date versions of the software.

Table 4-4. *Versions of current Windows operating systems with BitLocker support*

Windows 10	Education, Professional, or Enterprise edition
Windows 8	Professional or Enterprise edition
Windows 7	Enterprise or Ultimate edition

Now, let's implement a full-disk encryption scheme with **BitLocker**. Navigate to *System & Security* ➤ *BitLocker Drive Encryption* in Windows. Choose the drive you wish to encrypt (e.g., *Windows (C:)*) and click *Turn on BitLocker*. You will be presented with an unlocking option; you can choose either to *Enter a password* or to *Insert a USB-stick*.

Next, it's time to choose a way for storing the recovery key. You'll have the alternatives of using your Microsoft account, saving the recovery key to another USB device, saving it into a file, or printing it out on a piece of paper.

We'll now get to choose how much of the drive will be encrypted. You can select to encrypt either only the files already in use or to cover the entire hard drive. In general, the latter is the slower, but safer option.

It's at this point when installing BitLocker on Windows 10 you get the option of using the XTS-AES operating mode, referred on this screen as *New encryption mode*. If you're encrypting a movable storage device, such as a USB-stick, it's best to choose *Compatible mode* instead.

Finally, BitLocker will want to check your drive for errors and restart Windows to begin the encryption process, which will run smoothly in the background. If you need to get some work done or even shut down your computer, you can do it safely even at this stage of BitLocker's operation.

The preceding example, while providing us with a robustly encrypted operating system, didn't take into account the various hardware-based security measures previously mentioned in the chapter. All of that will be covered later in the book.

Linux Unified Key Setup (LUKS)

Most current distributions of Linux offer a robust encryption standard, the *Linux Unified Key Setup*, created by one *Clemens Fruhwirth* and released in 2004. A very versatile system, LUKS offers three varieties of AES encryption in addition to many others. It allows for full-disk encryption, too. LUKS is used in conjunction with *cryptsetup*, a tool for creating and managing encrypted disks and partitions in Linux.

LUKS allows multiple users to decrypt the master key. Unlike the other two OS-based encryption approaches mentioned in this chapter, LUKS is open source. Backdoors aren't therefore an issue. This makes LUKS a great choice for Top Secret tier material; only extraterrestrials and that guy with peanut allergy in the cafeteria might be able to access disks encrypted with it.

Now, LUKS is potentially one of the safest system-wide encryption techniques mentioned in this chapter, certainly more so than Apple's or Microsoft's products, simply due to the transparency it offers. We'll be looking into LUKS with much more attention later in this book. For now, it suffices you're aware of it.

Third-Party Encryption Suites

Naturally, encryption built into operating systems aren't your only solution for any cryptographic needs you may have. The scene of third encryption software is vibrant and chock-full of great products. We'll take a look at few of the most useful software in this category next (see Table 4-5).

Table 4-5. *A summary of some popular third-party encryption tools*

Software	OS Support	Pre-boot Authentication	Full-Disk Encryption	TPM Support
BestCrypt	Windows, MacOS, Linux (partial)	Yes	Yes	Yes
DriveCrypt	Windows	Yes	Yes	No
eCryptfs	Linux	No	No	Yes
ProxyCrypt	Windows	No	Yes	No
VeraCrypt	Windows, MacOS, Linux	For Windows only	Yes	No

BestCrypt by Jetico

Full-disk encryption (FDE) in Jetico's line of products, called *BestCrypt Volume Encryption*, gives you a choice of five encryption algorithms, all running on their most secure mode of 256-bit keys and all operating on XTS. While offering dual-operating system support (i.e., Windows and MacOS), FDE in BestCrypt only supports hardware-based security measures (i.e., TPM) for users of Windows. BestCrypt doesn't have an FDE product for Linux.

However, Jetico also offers a separate file container-based product for Windows, MacOS, and Linux each; this is called the *BestCrypt Container Encryption*.

In 2013, Jetico released the full source code for its encryption products (i.e., the *BestCrypt Development Kit*); it's very unlikely this software comes with any backdoors. One could do a lot worse than to purchase a BestCrypt license for their organization. A 21-day free trial is available on the Jetico website as of this writing.

Download BestCrypt here: **www.jetico.com**.

DiskCryptor by ntldr

Although last updated in 2014, *DiskCryptor* is a stable and secure open source solution for nearly impenetrable encryption. Made exclusively for Windows, the software comes with AES and two other algorithms which can also be used in tandem with each other.

DiskCryptor is highly optimized for Intel's core line of processors, but due to its design approach, it's very fast on other types of CPUs as well.

The author of DiskCryptor quite correctly assumes that commercial encryption solutions, while technically impressive, do have major issues. Clunky interfaces aside, open source cryptography is ultimately the way to go as we will see later in the book.

Download DiskCryptor here: **https://diskcryptor.net**.

DriveCrypt by SecurStar

Advertised as "military strength encryption," DriveCrypt's 1344-bit key strength sounds quite robust indeed. As for its algorithms, the software offers about a half a dozen including AES and, rather interestingly, the obsolete DES. How exactly the massive key strength is obtained is unclear, but on paper DriveCrypt seems like a solid Windows-only encryption solution. The software even features support for advanced steganography (as discussed earlier in the book) which is the technique of hiding sensitive data in plain daylight in the form of fake music files and the like.

As for backdoors, SecurStar remain adamant that these are not included in their products. Based in Germany, their claim seems to carry some heft as the country is quite comfortable with cryptographic freedoms. This may or may not change in the future, and if it does, SecurStar have vowed to "move the company accordingly."

A free 30-day demo version of DriveCrypt is available as of this writing.

Download DriveCrypt here: **www.securstar.com/en/drivecrypt.html**.

eCryptfs

Not a software suite per se, *eCryptfs* is in fact a complete cryptographic file system for Linux. This solution is actually a so-called *stacked file system*, which refers to eCryptfs co-operating with a Linux file system. It has been a part of the Ubuntu distribution since version 9.04. It's also included in Google's *Chrome* Operating System, which is a Linux variant.

eCryptfs adds cryptographic metadata into files, so that any encrypted files can be easily transmitted between hosts. These files will be then decrypted automatically should the proper key/password be in the Linux keyring. eCryptfs utilizes the AES algorithm.

As with most things Linux, eCryptfs is open source and not likely to have backdoors. A tad complicated for beginners, this is a powerful cryptographic tool in the arsenal of any organization in need of additional reinforcement into their security regime.

Download eCryptfs here: **https://ecryptfs.org**.

ProxyCrypt by v77

Described by its author as a tool for "paranoids and advanced users," ProxyCrypt is a powerful open source encryption system. On offer are three algorithms, including the 256-bit variety of AES. Available for Windows only, ProxyCrypt is a somewhat obscure piece of software but is both speedy and secure. It's a great choice for a robust full-disk encryption solution with features such as hardware acceleration and automatic key stretching (a technique discussed in the previous chapter).

Although ProxyCrypt was first released in 2013, it is a command-line tool, meaning it uses a sparse text-based approach. However, a free graphical user interface is available, which makes the software more appealing to beginners.

Download ProxyCrypt here: **https://sourceforge.net/projects/ proxycrypt**.

VeraCrypt by IDRIX

Based on the legacy of a once very popular cryptographic system, *TrueCrypt (2004–2011)*, *VeraCrypt* is an open source, feature-rich encryption suite available for Windows, MacOS, and Linux. Extensively audited and deemed to be without backdoors, you can use this fine piece of software for either full-disk encryption or for container files.

VeraCrypt offers five individual encryption algorithms, including AES, as well as their ten different combinations. It uses the XTS mode of operation and has full support for hardware-based acceleration (i.e., AES-NI). Also, if you have old TrueCrypt file containers somewhere you still want to access, VeraCrypt allows for that, too. Do note that the developers of VeraCrypt are vehemently opposed to adding support for trusted platform modules, as they feel a potential physical visit from a malicious party would negate the benefits of any TPM-devices.

Download VeraCrypt here: **www.veracrypt.fr/en/Home.html**.

Tutorial Time!

Knowing how much theory goes into encryption, it might surprise you how comfortable much of current-generation cryptographic software is to use. We'll now create a secure file container which may or may not be your very first one. For this task we'll be using the outstanding VeraCrypt tool.

1. **Download VeraCrypt from the URL provided before.**

2. **Install and run the software**. You'll arrive at the main VeraCrypt window (see Figure 4-1).

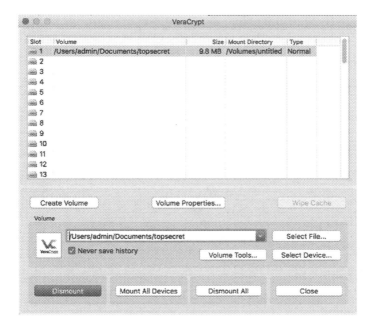

Figure 4-1. *The main VeraCrypt-window*

It is here we get to create and access our encrypted
file containers. You'll notice the software offers you
a total of 64 slots. This is the maximum amount
of file containers you can operate on at the same
time. However, you might only need a slot or
two, depending on the size of your operation/
organization. Next, we'll proceed to create a new
container called *topsecret* (which is already visible in
Figure 4-1).

3. **Click Create Volume**. You'll be given two options.
   Choose *Create an encrypted file container* and click
   Next.

4. **On the next prompt, choose *Standard VeraCrypt volume*** and click Next.

5. **Click Select file and navigate to the folder you want our file container to reside in.**

6. **Review Encryption options**. The defaults are set to AES as the encryption algorithm and SHA-256 as the hashing method. These are both fine choices, so let's just click *Next*.

7. **Decide on the volume size**. You can enter the file container size in kilobytes, megabytes, or gigabytes. For our purposes, let's choose the nice round number of ten megabytes and click *Next*.

8. **Enter key/password.** VeraCrypt wisely informs us about the importance of good passwords. A password which isn't directly taken from the dictionary and is at least 20 characters in length is highly recommended. A good password would be something like *iuyERwuy8321!53tNbv_*. A bad one would be *hello123*. A really bad one would be *hello*. Should you enter an atrocious password at this stage, the software will inform you of this and suggest you come up with a better one post haste. After you've decided on a password, click *Next*.

Note   If you ever regret your choice of passwords in VeraCrypt, you can change them later from the main window by choosing a mounted file container and clicking Volume Tools ➤ Change Volume Password.

---

9. **Select format options**. This setting depends on
    which operating system you intend to access the file
    container. Both FAT and exFAT are compatible in
    Windows, MacOS, and Linux.

10. **Decide on cross-platform support**. If you chose
    a file system other than FAT, a prompt will appear
    warning you about the dangers of having an OS-
    specific file system. You can then choose to either go
    back to step 9 and choose differently or stubbornly
    proceed with the choice you previously made.

11. **Move your mouse around the VeraCrypt window**.
    Seriously, do this until the blue bar reaches
    its rightmost edge. This step uses user mouse
    movement to add a degree of randomness to the
    encryption at hand.

12. **Click Format**. Your file container is now being
    created in the location you chose in step 5. This
    process might take quite a lengthy amount of time,
    depending on how big a container you chose to
    create and the processing power your computer has.

13. **Click Select file on the VeraCrypt main window**.
    Navigate to the directory where you chose to store
    the file container. Click Mount. You'll be now asked
    for the password. After another potentially long
    wait, the file container is now recognized by your OS
    and you can start adding files into it.

Congratulations! You have now taken your first steps in digital cryptography. Keep those mankini and/or swimsuit shots safe. The preceding tutorial demonstrated how to use VeraCrypt, but many of the steps are similar to those in other third-party encryption products as well.

In Closing

After finishing this chapter, you will have hopefully gained awareness of the following:

- How operating systems organize data on storage devices, including what sectors and blocks refer to

- How different file systems relate to each other

- The basics of CBC and AES-XTS block cipher operating modes

- Which popular third-party cryptographic software titles are out there

- How to create and use file containers using the VeraCrypt tool

In the next chapter we'll discuss a whole host of cryptographic attacks, scams, and other seedy concepts. We'll naturally also cover how to best tackle each of these nefarious techniques. Take a deep breath and please, stand clear!

CHAPTER 5

Common Attacks Against Cryptographic Systems

As formidable and secure as a computer with strong encryption sounds, there is literally an entire scientific discipline for breaking into such systems. In this chapter we'll take a look at many of these malicious techniques designed for breaking into cryptographic systems. Also, we'll tackle many other cyberthreats which are not specifically related to cryptographic environments, such as malware and network-based attacks, as these often go hand in hand. We'll also introduce some concepts important for the topic at hand.

Remember, you don't have to be an expert in cryptographic attacks after finishing this chapter or book. It's enough that you roughly know what types of attacks are out there and how to defend against them. We'll revisit these threats in the next chapters.

© Robert Ciesla 2020
R. Ciesla, *Encryption for Organizations and Individuals*,
https://doi.org/10.1007/978-1-4842-6056-2_5

Cryptographic Attack Models

Let's say some malicious actor, we'll call him *Larry*, wants to either breach into a secure system or discover aspects of the key to decrypt it. For that, there are several different approaches, which depend on the type and amount of information Larry has. Here are the four typical so-called cryptographic attack models:

- **Ciphertext only**. Only the encrypted data is in Larry's possession. He could try a *brute-force attack*. This refers to the daunting task of guessing every possible password/key until the correct one is found and the encrypted data is decrypted.

- **Known plaintext**. Larry has at least some parts of both the encrypted data and the corresponding plaintext (i.e., the decrypted data).

- **Chosen plaintext**. Larry gains access to the encrypted system, but is unable to find the key/password. However, he can encrypt a number of randomly chosen plaintexts and use the resulting ciphertexts to deduce the key.

- **Chosen cipher text**. Larry gets to examine both a bunch of cipher texts and their plaintext counterparts. He may, for example, lure an unsuspecting system administrator into encrypting specific plaintexts and have him or her deliver them back as cipher text. Larry then attempts to use the results to eventually gain the password/key. This attack model works mostly against public-key encryption schemes, such as RSA.

In cryptography, an *attack vector*, or simply *vector*, refers to the approach a malicious actor takes against a system.

Cryptanalysis

Cryptanalysis is the analysis of information systems in order to gain information about potential hidden sets of data in these systems. The aforementioned four attack models are part and parcel of cryptanalysis. Modern cryptanalysis techniques date back to the early 1990s and they can be split roughly into two groups: linear and differential. These techniques will be discussed next. While both of them were originally devised to thwart the now obsolete DES cipher (as discussed in Chapter 1), they are still relevant to this day.

Linear Cryptanalysis

Cryptographer *Mitsuru Matsui* introduced *linear cryptanalysis* in 1993. With this approach, a malicious actor seeks to find linear relations between a few bits from the plaintext (i.e., the unencrypted dataset), the encrypted message, and the so-called round keys we discussed in Chapter 3 in the context of the AES algorithm. Linear cryptanalysis uses a *known plaintext attack model* (see the "Cryptographic Attack Models" section earlier in this chapter).

Differential Cryptanalysis

Contrast to linear cryptanalysis, *differential cryptanalysis* is used not only against block ciphers (e.g., AES) but also cryptographic hash functions. This technique is usually attributed to cryptographers *Eli Biham* and *Adi Shamir* sometime in the late 1980s. Differential cryptanalysis is a *chosen-plaintext attack model* (see the "Cryptographic Attack Models" section). Under this scenario we have access to the encrypted system, but not the password.

Basically, differential cryptanalysis is used to examine how differences in the data input affect the output in a cryptographic event; the technique is looking for instances of nonrandom data in a cipher. This can ultimately result in the discovery of the secret key/password for decrypting an entire dataset.

Birthday Attack

When attacking *hash values* (as discussed in Chapter 3), a malicious actor can choose to use the *birthday attack*. Let's say a hash value is 64 bits in length, so its possible values span $1.8x10^{19}$, a fairly large range. However, after repeatedly evaluating a function with different input data, the exact same output is expected to be obtained after only $5.1x10^9$ instances of input. If the attacker is able to find two different inputs that give the exact same hash value, a collision event has occurred and the hash function in question has been broken. Birthday attacks are in essence a form of the *brute-force attack*, which we will get into next.

Brute-Force Attack (BFA)

Perhaps the most basic of cryptographic attacks, a *brute-force attack* simply refers to a malicious actor entering as many potential passwords into a system hoping one of them unlocks it. This type of attack is mostly useful against weak (i.e., short and/or trivial) passwords and as of decades ago, fully automated.

While not very efficient when executed by humans, a dedicated brute-force computer can theoretically enter millions of passwords per second into a system. Also, more technologically complicated approaches exist, such as chaining several computers together to create a more or less formidable brute-force task force. However, as of 2020, brute-force attacks are usually of limited use for malicious actors due to public awareness of strong passwords and various automated countermeasures.

Also, there's a so-called reverse brute-force attack, which refers to the process of entering common passwords into multiple user accounts in the hope that the owners of at least some of these accounts didn't choose strong passwords, opting for "password1" or a similar, disgraceful key instead.

Countermeasures Against Brute-Force Attack:

- Limiting the amount of passwords one can enter into a system per session

- Using strong passwords (12 characters minimum, no words from a dictionary, including special characters such as *!"#_%&*)

- Implementing *Completely Automated Public Turing test to tell Computers and Humans Apart (CAPTCHA)* to protect against automated attacks (see Figure 5-1)

Figure 5-1. *A CAPTCHA system in action*

The **Turing test**, created by famous computer scientist *Alan Turing (1912–1954),* refers to a computer's ability to fool a human being so that they feel they are communicating with a fellow member of the homo sapiens species. This can be implemented as, say, a (more or less) intelligent chat program. As of 2020, there are very few examples of this in existence.

Contact Analysis

Related to frequency analysis as presented in Chapter 1, *contact analysis* is an attack which examines which characters (e.g., letters or numbers) precede or follow other characters. In any language (e.g., English), certain characters share adjacency more than others.

Although mostly relegated to classical cryptography, contact analysis can be utilized in some modern contexts as a type of *ciphertext only* attack (see "Cryptographic Attack Models" section). Contact analysis is based on conditional probability, in which an event becomes possible should a certain condition be first met.

Best Countermeasure Against Contact Analysis:

- Forcing users to use complex passwords with special characters

Evil Maid Attack

An *evil maid attack* simply refers to an attack on an unattended device. A malicious actor with physical access alters a device in some nearly undetectable way so that they can later access the device and the data on it. Never let that one suspicious maid or roommate sneak up on your devices; guard them well!

Countermeasures Against Evil Maid Attack:

- Video surveillance on critical premises 24/7

- Locked doors and/or more-or-less armed guards

Heuristic Attack

A part of many cryptographic attacks, the *heuristic attack* simply consists of a malicious actor using well-established password-enhancement practices preferred by many. Users often opt to add numbers either to the beginning or the end of their passwords, hoping it will make it more resistant to attacks (e.g., *"password"* vs. *"password123"* or *"123password"*). While somewhat better than a simple dictionary-picked password, a more effective approach is to ditch the dictionary altogether.

Countermeasures Against Heuristic Attacks:

- Do not enter numbers in sequences into your passwords (e.g., *hello123*).

- Go for more obscure symbols when it comes to your key security (e.g., *%&/^*).

Man-in-the-Middle (MITM)

Man-in-the-middle is a type of attack where an attacker secretly delivers and potentially tampers with the communications between two parties who are unaware of said attacker's actions. The malicious actor might be able to fully convince either or both parties they are sending data to each other. We are not only talking about tampering with mail or messages. Man-in-the-middle attacks can take place on a binary level where, instead of two human parties, an attacker can convince a device or system that he or she is the legitimate party to send its data to.

There are two major defensive strategies against man-in-the-middle attacks: *authentication* and *tampering detection*. Encrypted systems with robust authentication (i.e., SSL/TLS) are virtually immune to these types of attacks. The technique of tampering detection focuses on anomalies in latency.

Countermeasures Against Man-in-the-Middle Attacks:

- Utilizing exclusively public-key (i.e., asymmetric) encryption, such as RSA or ElGamal

- Relying only on trusted third-party certificates with SSL/TLS

Meet-in-the-Middle

Not to be confused with man-in-the-middle, a *meet-in-the-middle attack* is used in environments where an encryption algorithm using multiple layers and keys has been implemented. Put simply, in this type of attack, a malicious actor targets both the plaintext and the ciphertext simultaneously, hoping to "meet in the middle" of a dataset to decrypt it. This is a known plaintext attack (see the "Cryptographic Attack Models" section).

A mostly theoretical threat, meet-in-the-middle works best in scenarios such as international or corporate espionage. It could be described as the bigger, more cantankerous brother of the brute-force attack. This type of attack is a good reason why ciphers like the *Triple DES,* as robust as they sound, may not be ideal choices after all. Also, meet-in-the-middle attacks can be difficult to detect; therefore, prevention is the way to go.

Countermeasures Against Meet-in-the-Middle Attacks:

- Installing an either software- or hardware-based *intrusion detection system (IDS).* As efficient as these solutions can be, they are also prone to give false alarms. Although similar to traditional firewalls, an IDS is not the same thing.

- Steering clear of algorithms such as Double or Triple DES which use multiple keys and encryption phases.

Rainbow Table Attack

A *rainbow table* is a database used to facilitate breaking passwords' hash values. It's basically a dictionary consisting of passwords and their hashes. A rainbow table is more time-effective than many other cryptographic attacks, especially those of the brute-force variety, as all of its hash values used are precalculated. Rainbow tables were discovered by cryptographer *Philippe Oechslin*.

Many online service providers only store password hashes on their servers and not the keys themselves. So an exact password needn't be extracted; whenever hash values match, the transaction is authenticated.

A crucial concept in cryptanalysis, a *time-memory trade-off* simply means the malicious parties' prioritization of a system's memory-related resources over time-related ones – or vice versa.

As dreamy as rainbow tables sound from a malicious actor's perspective, they have some disadvantages. Namely, a robust rainbow table can eat up a hefty piece of storage media. Under some circumstances, they may include the hash value of nearly every imaginable password, after all.

One of the most notorious tools in the world of rainbow tables is a piece of software called *RainbowCrack*, devised by cryptographer *Zhu Shuanglei*. Operating in the Microsoft Windows and Linux environments, the tool even supports video card (i.e., GPU) accelerated processing for quite a cryptanalytical punch.

Countermeasures Against Rainbow Table Attacks:

- Users: pick strong (i.e., long and complicated) passwords only. System administrators: choose to implement newer and more secure hashing algorithms, such as *SHA-256* or *SHA-3*. Also, secure your hash value database with every means at your disposal, including budgeting for physical security.

- Salting and/or peppering as described in Chapter 3 (e.g., adding random data to hash values and passwords). This is usually a rather devastating response against these types of attacks.

- Implementing *key stretching*, which refers to adding multiple passes of salted hash data into the hash function.

Replay Attack

A *replay attack* is a type of simple man-in-the-middle or eavesdropping approach. This type of attack consists of a malicious party retransmitting valid credentials into a system, thereby gaining access to it. In theory, a replay attack can be therefore used to circumvent even the strongest of encryption schemes.

Countermeasures Against Replay Attacks:

- Using a *session ID* approach, where each run of a program is assigned a random, one-time token; a malicious party simply couldn't replicate this to commence a replay attack later.

- Using *timestamps*, where "the lines are open" only for a brief time window.

Related Key Attack

Whenever a malicious actor can observe multiple keys/passwords being used in a cryptographic context, he or she may be eventually able to decrypt a secure system. This is done by discovering mathematical consistencies between the data in the keys and is called a *related key attack*. This is mostly a theoretical threat especially against newer encryption algorithms like the AES.

Best countermeasure Against Related Key Attacks:

- Using random-key generation approaches, such as a *key derivation function (KDF)*. A KDF derives multiple keys, whenever desired, from a single *master key* using a pseudorandom function.

In cryptography, a *pseudorandom function (PRF)* refers to one of the most robust means of generating random numbers. It's not the same as a *pseudorandom generator (PRG)*. A PRG offers a **single output** at random if the **input** was chosen at random. Now, with a PRF **all** of its outputs seem random regardless of how the corresponding inputs were chosen.

Rubber-Hose Attack

Perhaps the crudest type of cryptanalysis, *rubber-hose attacks* refer to subjecting the owner of a key/password to coercion or physical violence to extract said information. Cryptography isn't always diplomatic. We'll be looking at legal aspects and the rights of password holders in Chapter 7.

Countermeasures Against Rubber-Hose Attacks:

- Staying out of countries with poor human rights records

- Choosing your friends carefully

Side Channel Attack (SCA)

A *side channel attack* doesn't utilize any weaknesses in a system, rather it focuses on its actual implementation and what attack vectors that offers. There are several categories of side channel attacks including those based on timing of data transfer, data remanence, and electromagnetic leakage (see Table 5-1).

In theory, a successful side channel attack can bypass encryption of any strength as no cracking of the cryptographic scheme has to be attempted. It's a scary thought. Luckily effective countermeasures exist.

Table 5-1. *Some typical cryptographic side channel attacks*

Type	Area of Focus	Skill Level Required
Acoustic	Audio (e.g., user keystrokes)	High
Data remanence	Critical data left on storage media (e.g., hard drives)	Low
Electromagnetic (EMF)	EMF emissions from computer monitors	High
Optical	Visual sightings of target system components, advanced photon analysis	Low/high
Power analysis	Changes in a device's electricity usage	High
Timing	A system's internal data transfers	High

Countermeasures Against Side Channel Attacks (SCAs):

Due to the nature and wide variety of SCA attacks, you'll need a plethora of defensive strategies to counter them successfully; you should implement as many of these as you can. The following is an overview of these techniques. They will be discussed in more detail in the next chapters.

- **Acoustic SCAs** not only involve keyboard noises, but in some cases also sounds emitted by computer hardware, such as sounds from the CPU and hard drives. These can be used to deduce information about an encrypted system potentially compromising it.

  For these types of attacks, a complete soundproofing solution with a *white noise generator* should be installed in critical locations. White noise is a type of random audio signal with equal intensity at different frequencies, familiar to some as "static" and similar to an untuned radio.

- **Electromagnetic SCAs** focus on detecting patterns in the electromagnetic radiation emitted by electronic devices using specialized hardware and software. These attacks may be quite hard to detect as they are by nature un-invasive.

  Electromagnetic SCAs, including government TEMPEST attacks, can be almost completely defeated by a *Faraday cage*; this is an isolation chamber used for blocking electromagnetic fields invented by *Michael Faraday* back in 1836. You can isolate fairly large areas from EMF signals with these cages and fill them with any kind of device, and personnel, you feel like; they are quite safe for human use. Also, Faraday cages can be used to protect against Mother Nature's lightning attacks.

87

- Distance works well to decrease the amount of data a bad actor can gather using these types of attacks. Keeping a wide, secure perimeter around your servers and/or workstations may do the trick.

TEMPEST (Telecommunications Electronics Materials Protected from Emanating Spurious Transmissions) is an NSA specification dealing with data leakage through radio waves, vibration, EMF, or sound. It covers both the attack and defense aspects of this phenomenon.

- **Data remanence SCAs** can be dealt with rather simple means. A free, third-party disk eraser/wiper software will suffice in most cases. Several effective wiping algorithms have been devised over the years; mere file deletion or drive formatting does not suffice. Deleted files, whether encrypted or not, can linger in an operating system for weeks before being overwritten by new data. Again, formatting the drive will also not usually guarantee all critical files are permanently erased.

  For a long time, the de facto algorithm for secure file wiping was the *US Department of Defense standard 5220.22-M*, which uses a three-step process for erasing data. First, a mass storage device is filled with binary zeros. This is followed by writing it full of binary ones. Finally, it's filled with random patterns of binary data. With the advent of solid-state drives (SSDs), this approach is no longer considered up to par. However, the DoD standard still works for traditional hard drives for the most part.

SSD devices should be erased with specialized software, usually provided by the drive manufacturer (e.g., Samsung or OCZ). Other data wiping software generally only works traditional, mechanical hard drives.

For truly vigorous data destruction, one can physically decimate hard drives and other forms of mass media by, say, dropping them into a steel mill blast furnace – or volcano. Simply hammering or breaking apart a hard drive may not be enough to guarantee the data isn't recoverable as there are very advanced (although expensive) laboratories that can reassemble a shattered drive in no time.

- **Optical SCAs** range from simple hidden high-resolution video cameras to advanced, usually government-provided devices which actually spy on photons inside a computer to deduce information; the latter scenario should only concern you if you're working at a very shady organization indeed.

  The detection and removal of hidden cameras, which may be extremely small as of 2020, naturally works fine against the simpler variety of optical SCAs.

  You should invest in special darkened screens for all of your monitors to further hinder any spying attempts from dubious visitors to your premises.

- With **power analysis SCAs**, one can deduce which mathematical operation a device is processing, in binary digits (i.e., zeros or ones), by tracing a processor's power use patterns. This is known to work for figuring out data encrypted with older algorithms, such as the RSA, as well as the de facto AES. Tools like digital oscilloscopes are used for this type of attack. Now, there are a variety of both hardware- and software-based countermeasures against this subset of SCAs.

- Power analysis SCAs can be made more difficult by implementing *electronic filters* which attenuate the detectable signals to a bare minimum; this hinders the ability of an oscilloscope to detect elements detrimental to a cryptographic system. These filters can be either passive, consisting of analog electronic components, or active (i.e., based on amplifying parts requiring external power).

- *Power-line filters* work to reduce the power supply noise found in most electronic systems. This technique can even out the peaks and valleys in a signal needed for a successful power trace.

- When it comes to the software side of things, randomness is your friend. Injecting a signal with random instructions from a microcontroller can confuse an attacker and provide a good additional layer to your cryptographic security.

- S-box (i.e., substitution-box) operations found in algorithms like the AES don't need to be performed in any specific order (see Chapter 3 for a reminder on this phase in a round of AES). Putting these operations in a random order is therefore beneficial. This technique will either completely thwart an attack or at least greatly add to the amount of resources an attacker needs to break into a system. *S-box shuffling* is also very time- and energy-efficient, more so than the approach of adding random instructions into the proceedings.

- **Timing SCAs** examine the delays in cryptographic operations. Different algorithms may have recognizable characteristics which can be exploited to compromise a cryptosystem. However, malicious actors attempting this type of attack usually need detailed information on the system such as the make of the CPU/processor and the overall system design paradigm being used.

- Timing SCAs can be foiled, in select cases, by keeping the hardware internals of a system hidden. The technique is known as *security through obscurity*, which has been a widely rejected approach since the nineteenth century. Skilled malicious actors can discover the makeup of any hardware rather trivially in no time.

- *Blinding* is a technique which can protect an asymmetric cryptographic system (i.e., a public-key scheme such as RSA or ElGamal) against timing SCAs. In this context blinding works to add random elements into an algorithm's input which are not entirely known by any single party. There are several ways to implement cryptography-related blinding and some are more efficient than others.

Cyberthreats Not Specific to Cryptography

We'll now explore some common threats not specifically designed against encrypted systems. As mighty as they seem, encrypted systems aren't immune to any of these attacks; when a nonmalicious user has entered the right password and booted up a computer, online malware is as serious a threat as on a completely nonencrypted system.

Malware

A portmanteau for "malicious software," *malware* is simply any type of software which causes harm to a system, from minor annoyances to taking full control. Any organization, minor or major, can be taken down with a clever enough malware. Now, there are numerous types of malware, some of which we'll go through next.

Trojan Horse

Named after the ancient Greek story, a *Trojan horse* is at first a seemingly harmless piece of software which turns out to be bona fide malware when executed. Often, Trojan horses are presented as innocent or even useful downloads in the form of email attachments from an unknown actor, a fake software update, or a fraudulent advertisement on a website.

Not all Trojan horses are created by your average hackers; many governments actually use them as a form of cyber-warfare and espionage.

Keylogger

Basically, this type of malware exists to collect users' keystrokes to gather usernames, passwords, or other information useful to the attacker (such as financial information). Needless to say, this can entail a whole host of issues from hijacked social media accounts to online banking trouble. Most keyloggers are software-based, although hardware-based units also exist. There are also some advanced ones which actually use an open microphone and an acoustic analysis to deduce which keys were pressed.

Man-in-the-Browser (MITB)

This type of threat takes over a web browser using its potential vulnerabilities. It's a remote Trojan horse able to modify the contents of web pages from the user's perspective. Worst of all, an MITB is capable of interfering with online bank transfers and the amounts of currency they process. In fact, this type of attack is considered one of the worst threats to secure online banking, since it's often completely invisible to the user.

Boy-in-the-Browser (BITB)

A smaller-scale version of the man-in-the-browser attack also exists, called the *boy-in-the-browser attack*. BITBs target visitors to specific malicious websites. A type of malware is forcefully installed to change a user's computer's network traffic to become a part of a man-in-the-middle attack in the online realm. After the damage has been done, the program might delete itself, making its detection nearly impossible.

Botnet

Consisting of a large number of connected devices and functioning online, a *botnet* is in essence a centrally controlled "army" of said devices usually used for malicious purposes. A bot refers to an infected computer or smartphone. Botnets can yield a lot of digital leverage and can consists of millions of bots; the user may not even be aware that his or her device has been compromised. For one, email spammers love their botnets. Also, they are used to distribute Trojan horses and other malware online.

Infected systems that are a part of a botnet are usually called *zombie computers*.

Distributed Denial-of-Service (DDoS) Attack

One of the most common and frustrating attacks an organization can face is an attack called *distributed denial of service*. This online offense is executed using large botnets which exhaust a website of its resources, resulting in the whole site crashing down and offering very little apart from an error message to its visitors. This can be devastating for critical businesses dealing in online banking, health care, and others. In 2012 six major US banks, including *Bank of America*, experienced issues thanks to a large-scale distributed denial-of-service attack. A smaller-scale variety of this attack, *denial of service (DoS)*, exists; these may target smaller organizations from time to time. Attacks of this type often originate from a smaller number of sources.

Phishing Attack

Whenever a malignant piece of software or website poses as a legitimate party, it's called *phishing*. A very popular type of cyber-scam, this kind of attack is used to "fish" for usernames, passwords, credit card numbers, and other sensitive data from unsuspecting users thinking they're dealing with genuine businesses.

General-purpose mass phishing aside, there are several more unique techniques for this attack. *Whaling* refers to targeting high-profile targets, such as politicians or corporate executives. This type of approach can take the form of a well-written subpoena or other legal document and often results in sensitive data or a hefty sum of money sliding into the hands of a malicious actor. Any critical data obtained from a high-profile individual is naturally worth quite a tad in the black market. Whaling is sometimes also referred to as *business email compromise (BEC)*.

One of the biggest examples of whale phishing was the 2016 incident when the then-presidential candidate *Hillary Clinton's* campaign head *John Podesta* was tricked to hand over his email account password by malicious actors. The phishing email simply told Podesta his Gmail account had been hacked (by actors in Ukraine, no less) and that he needed to change the password – by clicking a detrimental link.

Spear phishing is simply the malicious act of using a personalized approach for gaining information or financial gain. The social media revolution fueled this type of attack due to the considerable amount of individuals who release a large amount of data about their lives on a daily basis. A spear phisher may pose as a person's colleague, friend, or even spouse to extract money or other resources.

Possibly the hardest to detect, *clone phishing* is the act of intercepting legitimate communications, such as email, and injecting it with a malicious attachment, message, or link. An email may seem to originate from a perfectly legitimate party but was in fact tampered with by a malicious third party. Usually the bad sender's email address is either a variation of the original sender's address or a straight-up nonsensical one; always pay attention to these details.

Bad actors on their way into the world of phishing benefit greatly from the so-called phishing kits. These are basically more or less authentic-looking duplicates of websites by well-known businesses, such as Facebook, Apple, or Microsoft. Combined with large mailing lists, perhaps obtained from the seedier parts of the Internet, these kits offer many potential victims for wannabe cybercriminals. Faked websites using phishing kits tend to last a very short period of time online. However, in a span of 24 hours or even less, these sites can inflict a great deal of harm to a plethora of individuals and organizations; new ones are created on a daily, if not on an hourly, basis.

Lastly, there's yet another type of phishing attack known as *pharming*, which deals with the faking of *Domain Name Service (DNS)* entries. This is the technology which translates *Internet Protocol (IP)* addresses (e.g., *84.234.64.207*) preferred by electronic devices into something more pleasant to the human eye (e.g., *robertciesla.com*). Pharming transports a user, who entered a perfectly legitimate website address, into a malicious site dedicated for harvesting personal information. In some cases, these imitation sites are relatively easy to spot due to grammatical mistakes or other design flaws. A pharming site can also be visually perfectly similar when compared to its legitimate counterpart.

The various types of phishing attacks aren't limited to fake emails and websites. Cybercriminals use the full range of tools at their disposal, such as social media platforms, instant messaging services, and even faked online advertisements. Stay alert and watch out for even the smallest of discrepancies in tone, design, and sender identity in all of your online communications.

Policeware

Many governments are known to spy on their citizens. There's a specialized type of software for this purpose which is often referred to as *policeware*. Once installed on a citizen's/suspect's computer, it can be very hard to detect and remove; many makers of anti-malware products may or may not have co-operated with law enforcement to guarantee this.

Perhaps the first large-scale example of policeware was *Carnivore* (later renamed *DCS1000*), devised by the FBI in the late 1990s and used primarily for email surveillance. It consisted of a Windows-based computer physically set up at a place of interest, usually at an *Internet Service Provider (ISP)* server room.

The FBI also created a software-based eavesdropping solution called *Magic Lantern*, first reported in 2001. A Trojan at heart, the software was/is usually distributed as an email attachment and it operates as a keylogger, for one.

More recently, the FBI have devised yet another piece of policeware called *Computer and Internet Protocol Address Verifier (CIPAV)*. The exact workings of this software aren't available, but it's said to collect a wide variety of information about the system it's installed on – and report back to the FBI. CIPAV is known to at least record any outbound communications, last visited website, type of operating system, and presently logged-in user account name. Hopefully mostly used to prevent crime, CIPAV has no place on a law-abiding citizen's computer.

Another somewhat notorious piece of surveillance software is called *FinFisher*. Surfacing sometime around 2011, it's been used by the governments of Canada, Egypt, Finland, Germany, India, and the United States, to name just six. FinFisher was created by *Gamma Group*, whose business shows no signs of declining. Human rights organizations worldwide have criticized the company's offerings, since they are used by several countries with lacking human rights records.

Rootkit

A very serious type of malware, *rootkits* mask themselves from the user – and most anti-malware software. Rootkits can be either automated, roaming the Internet looking for systems to compromise, or they can be installed by individual actors for any type of malicious purpose.

Some notorious rootkits include *Flame* (discovered in 2012), which was used for cyber-espionage in the Middle East, and *ZeroAccess* (discovered in 2011), which infected two million computers to create a massive botnet with them.

Even large corporations can be guilty of installing rootkits on the devices of their clientele. The biggest such case was the copy-protection scandal of 2005 coming from *Sony BMG*. Upon inserting a CD into a computer, a rootkit was silently installed on the system, greatly reducing its level of security against actual malware as well as eavesdropping on the usage habits of the user. The corporation first utilized a copy-protection scheme known as *Extended Copy Protection (XCP)* and later one known as *MediaMax CD-3*; both of these were basically malicious software.

While originally intended as a type of efficient copy-protection software, Sony BMG's rootkits compromised approximately 22 million users. This resulted in class-action lawsuits by litigators from the states of Texas, New York, and California.

Spyware

Closely related to policeware, *spyware* is pretty much the same thing – except it's usually coming from malicious, nongovernmental actors. Identity theft thrives from this type of malware; a person's identity and credit card numbers are well sought after among cybercriminals. Spyware usually operates fully covertly on an unsuspecting user's devices.

Credit card numbers aside, things that spyware can leak include usernames, passwords, financial records, and Internet browsing history. For purposes of blackmail, these types of malicious programs are often a cybercriminal's first choice. According to the *Federal Trade Commission (FTC)*, even back in 2003 more than 27.3 million Americans had been victims of identity theft of which a considerable portion was facilitated by spyware.

Virus

A *virus* is a type of self-replicating malware which can spread rapidly especially over online environments, potentially infecting tens of millions of computers and other devices. As of 2020 (and up until now), most viruses target Microsoft Windows operating systems. Since Windows is a very popular choice for organizations of all sizes, viruses cause financial losses of several billion dollars a year due to causing slowdowns, system crashes, and many other time-consuming scenarios. It's to be noted viruses do not self-execute; a user has to activate them.

Computer viruses can be thought of as a form of semi-intelligent artificial life. The first software program that ticks most of the boxes for being a virus was *The Creeper System* written by software developer *Bob Thomas* in 1971. However, the program did very little damage, simply displaying the message *"I'm the creeper: catch me if you can"* on infected computers of the time.

Signs your system may be infected with a virus/malware include a more sluggish computer, the introduction of software you never installed on your desktop, a browser home page you can't reset, and strange email sent from your email account(s). Other symptoms include annoying pop-ups and sudden shutdowns of your favorite programs.

Worm

Closely related to a virus is a *worm*, which is simply not only self-replicating but also automatically spreading and self-executing type of malicious software. Worms often spread through email and don't need any user interaction to activate themselves. They are among the most dangerous form of malware (see Table 5-2).

Table 5-2. *Some well-known worms and other types of malicious software from recent years*

Name	Type	Year Found	OS Affected	Damage Caused
Flashback	Trojan Horse	2011	MacOS	Harvested usernames & passwords
StuxNet	Worm	2010	Windows	Possibly ruined one-fifth of Iran's nuclear centrifuges
MyDoom	Email-worm	2004	Windows	Cost $38 billion to businesses
ILOVEYOU	Email-worm	2000	Windows	Damaged countless users' files
Bliss	Virus	1997	Linux	Demonstrated Linux isn't immune to viruses (being mostly harmless)

Ransomware

As a combination of a Trojan horse and a forced encryption of one's computer, *ransomware* is extremely dangerous and almost impossible to crack. Once the user executes an innocent-seeming file (i.e., the Trojan horse), the malware encrypts the system and prompts the user to pay a sum of money to have it decrypted (see Figure 5-2). Around 181.5 million ransomware attacks took place in the first six months of 2018 alone.

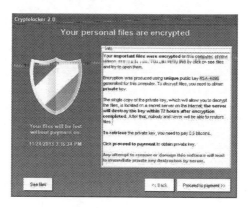

Figure 5-2. *A prompt from the notorious Cryptolocker ransomware*

There are plenty of lower-tier ransomware programs out there which can be removed with some know-how, but more advanced varieties of ransomware are only theoretically disposed of. Never execute, or allow your colleagues to execute, programs you're not absolutely comfortable with.

In Closing

After finishing this chapter, you will have hopefully gained awareness of the following:

- The main four cryptographic attack models

- What linear and differential cryptanalysis refer to

- The basics of the most common attacks against cryptographic systems and which countermeasures work best against them

- What various types of malware there are and the basics of their operation

In the next chapter we'll take a good gander at how to create near impenetrable contemporary systems using encryption and other approaches.

CHAPTER 6

Creating Extremely Secure Encrypted Systems

Like you may remember, in Chapter 4 we took a quick glance at encryption solutions for three of the most popular operating systems as of 2020: Microsoft Windows, MacOS, and Linux. In this chapter we'll not only expand on this topic, but also cover the best general security measures available for these operating systems in detail. We'll tackle the best anti-malware and other related solutions of today, in both software and hardware. After all, there's no effective cryptography without defensive technologies against every variety of serious malware. Feel free to implement as many of these countermeasures as you can.

Due to the possibility of backdoors, in this chapter we'll also have a focus on open source solutions for all software presented. Closed-source encryption software will still be featured as it does have its uses, even when/if backdoored.

© Robert Ciesla 2020
R. Ciesla, *Encryption for Organizations and Individuals*,
https://doi.org/10.1007/978-1-4842-6056-2_6

On Multilayer Encryption

As it stands, the mighty *Advanced Encryption Algorithm (AES)* is pretty much invincible until the unforeseeable future. Using a single layer of AES should be enough for even the most fervent cryptographers. However, there is an ongoing debate over the use of multilayered encryption. This approach and its associated concepts will be discussed next.

On the surface additional layers of encryption seem like great countermeasures against cryptographic attacks. Now, there are two schools of thought on this. Some proponents of multilayer encryption rightfully claim that in theory each additional implementation of an encrypting algorithm fortifies a dataset considerably. Others feel each such implementation only adds attack vectors for malicious actors to utilize. In addition, using numerous encryption algorithms simultaneously creates more strain on a system's resources, whether it seems negligible or not to involve human actors. Still, backdoors in closed-source commercial encryption products, such as Windows BitLocker, are a legitimate concern for many cryptographers.

Provided well-established algorithms such as AES are used, the biggest threat to a secure system lies in malicious software, often facilitated by human incompetence. This is why a large section of this chapter is dedicated to presenting the most effective countermeasures against malware known in 2020.

Whether one is suspicious of commercial encryption products or not, such a full-disk encryption is a great way to fend off data leaks obtained during burglaries and many forms of espionage. The government is unlikely to side with the offenders in these cases. Now, as demonstrated in Chapter 4, one solution against those pesky backdoors is to store your most delicate data within secure file containers. These should be naturally encrypted with open source solutions only, such as the much loved *VeraCrypt*. A double layer of, say, BitLocker and file containers consisting of another dose of 256-bit AES data is a tough nut to crack for any actor, whether highly skilled and malicious or not.

Now, should one implement multilayer encryption, some practices should be adhered to. For one, the passwords for each layer should be completely different and under no circumstance share patterns in any way. Also, weak algorithms for both encryption and hashing should be steered clear of. These include the *Digital Encryption Standard (DES)* in all of its varieties, as well as the *SHA-1* and *MD5*. The public-key mammoth that is the RSA algorithm, while not obsolete, doesn't represent the cutting edge in encryption any longer; it has some issues in both security and performance. Some cryptographers suggest either using RSA at its higher key sizes of 2048 bits (or more) or abandoning it altogether. Remember, the cryptographic quantum revolution is right around the corner as of 2020. Its first casualty may very well be algorithms like the once-venerable RSA.

Small vs. Big Business Readiness

While organizations of all sizes obviously need to implement proper security measures both online and in the traditional sense, there's often a different approach to these matters when it comes to smaller and established businesses. Larger enterprises have much more resources to spare, while the smaller actors tend to prioritize growth instead of security. This chapter is primarily for these less established business owners/ organizations, who may have not had the opportunity to outsource their cybersecurity solutions yet.

Now, eventually all organizations should have the following safeguards in place; and the sooner, the better:

- **A well-trained staff**. Your crew needs to be savvy to face the many threats the Internet throws at them. For one, bringing one's own online-capable devices into work may create issues with organizational security and should be addressed.

- **Update awareness.** Out-of-date security software is usually useless. Make sure yours doesn't get to that point. Apply reliable vendor patches whenever they arrive.

- **Secure B2B networks**. Even if your organization is up to speed when it comes to the latest in cybersecurity, doing business with a compromised party may infect your systems as well. The Internet at large is not the only potential infected agent. Care must be taken with robust protocols and digital hygiene must be considered in B2B communications as well.

- **Compartmentalization**. All data in your organization should be accessible on a need-to-know basis only. Only trusted IT staff should be granted with user accounts which allow software installation.

A Refresher on Network Security

Many cryptographic attack vectors are coming from an online environment. It makes sense to know at least the basics of current-day network hardware security which we'll delve into next.

Networks and Routers

Like you probably know, an interconnected series of devices sharing data using specific protocols constitutes a *network*. This can be a large corporate solution consisting of thousands of devices or a small home network consisting of exactly one router and a mere handful of devices, usually including a desktop computer (i.e., a typical *local area network*, or *LAN*). The Internet is basically one large network of servers and clients.

Now, a *router* is an important piece of hardware which transmits data between devices in a network. Website data, email, and other information coming in from the Internet enter a router in the form of *data packets*. All of these packets contain destination information (i.e., an *Internet protocol address* or *IP address*) which naturally belong to the device which made the request. Within a matter of seconds, these data packets find their way from the Internet into the router, which directs them toward a connected device.

There are a few important settings in routers which you need to pay close attention to; if such a device is compromised, it can infect a whole network, after all.

- **First, you need to access the router's console.** This is usually done by typing in a *default IP address* into a web browser on a device connected to the network (see Figure 6-1). There are a variety of these IP addresses as they vary between hardware manufacturers. A one-size-fits-all solution isn't unfortunately available. For example, some routers accept *192.168.1.1*, while others work with *192.168.0.1*.

- In addition to the default IP address, you also need a username and a password to access the router console. See Table 6-1 for some common combinations.

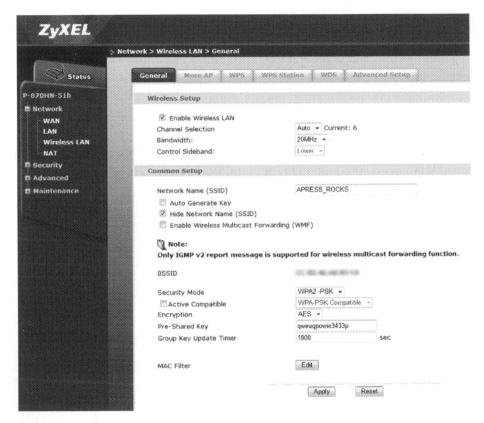

Figure 6-1. *A partial router console screen of a Zyxel-brand device*

Table 6-1. *Some common default router usernames and passwords as of Q2 2020*

Manufacturer	Default IP Address	Default Username	Default Password
Asus	192.168.1.1	admin	admin
Belkin	192.168.2.1	admin	admin
Digicom	192.168.1.254	admin	Michelangelo
Huawei/SUN/ZTE	192.168.0.1	admin	admin

(*continued*)

Table 6-1 . (*continued*)

Manufacturer	Default IP Address	Default Username	Default Password
Samsung	192.168.0.1	admin	password
Telco Systems	192.168.0.1	telco	telco
Zcom	192.168.0.1	root	admin
Zyxel	192.168.1.1	admin	1234

Usually the router's backside contains a sticker with the default username and password. If none of the preceding combinations work and/or you can't find the aforementioned sticker, refer to the manufacturer's website.

- **Next, you need to change the router's default password into a stronger one**. Remember the makings of a strong password: length, complexity, and not using a dictionary for inspiration.

- **When using Wi-Fi, make sure the strongest available encryption is in use.** Navigate to your router console's wireless page; it's usually listed under *Wireless LAN* or something to that effect.

- For your Wi-Fi encryption, you'll probably have the choice of *Wi-Fi Protected Access (WPA)* protocol in its three incarnations. The original WPA aside, you have the ubiquitous *WPA2* and, in the case of newer routers, the *WPA3* of 2018. While WPA2 has vulnerabilities, it's not practically obsolete like WPA. Always choose the latest possible version of this protocol.

- Many older network devices also offer *Wired Equivalent Privacy (WEP)* as an option. This standard was introduced in 1999 and came originally with mere 64-bit key length. WEP was later bolstered with 128- and 256-bit key lengths, but it remains a compromised protocol you should avoid. If your hardware only offers you this method for your Wi-Fi security, it's time to upgrade your routers.

- **Disable remote access and *Universal Plug and Play*.** The last thing you want is someone outside of your network to administer your router settings. In some devices remote access might enabled by default. Use the console to untick the box on this feature which is usually listed simply under *Remote Management* or *Remote MGMT*. Another feature you should seriously consider disabling is *Universal Plug and Play (uPnP)*. For one, a router with uPnP enabled may offer a method for hackers to bypass your device's firewall entirely.

- **Switch off *Wi-Fi Protected Setup (WPS)* as soon as you can.** This feature exists to facilitate a quick one-button solution for setting up a wireless network. Aimed mostly at the less geeky users, WPS is actually a major security problem in many cases. The system is implemented using either a four-digit PIN code or a push-button-connect approach. The latter is very susceptible to brute-force attacks, while having a malicious actor on the premises of your router neutralizes the former's effectiveness.

- **Get acquainted with network address translation (NAT).** This is a technique which takes a single public IP address and shares it with a multitude of connected devices using a router/firewall. For example, a router in a network might have the local IP of 192.168.1.1 and a public one of, say, 86.1.70.30 as assigned by your Internet service provider, visible for all the websites you or your employees visit using this setup. Now, under NAT the router will assign local IP addresses for any devices connected to it, for example, 192.168.1.2 for your desktop and 192.168.1.3 for your colleague's tablet (see Figure 6-2). These IP addresses will remain clandestine from the public at large.

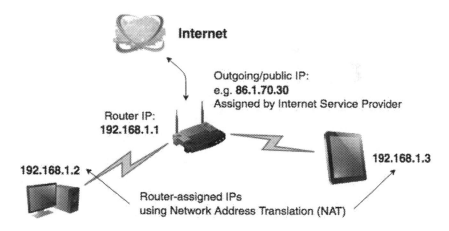

Figure 6-2. *A simple local area network using the NAT technique*

Better security aside, NAT allows for the conservation of limited amount of IPv4 addresses. Using a 32-bit address space, the IPv4 specification limits the global number of different public IP addresses to some 4.2 billion, still largely in use. Without unique IP addresses, the Internet can't function properly.

- How to make sure your router is running on NAT? Make sure the device uses *routing* instead of *bridging* for its mode of operation. This is usually the default setting. With bridging, you lose NAT in exchange for somewhat faster traffic flow; this is generally not recommended.

- **Update your router's firmware.** The firmware in a router is a writeable chunk of nonvolatile memory which holds the device's operating system. If you're running your device on old firmware, chances are you're either missing out on some good features or flat-out compromising your security. You'll find the latest firmware updates on your router's manufacturer's website usually under *Support* ➤ *Firmware*.

- **Make MAC filtering your best friend.** All networking devices, including routers and smartphones, have a unique *media access control (MAC)* address. It consists of six groups of hexadecimal values separated by colons and looks something like this: *b8:66:4c:f4:3d:6c*. For now, a MAC is allocated from a 48-bit address space. This allows for some 281 trillion unique strings and is designed to last us until 2080. A newer 64-bit implementation for MACs has been devised, but not yet widely adopted.

- *MAC filtering* is a technique where only safe hardware, identified through their unique MAC addresses, is allowed to access a local area network. In other words, a MAC filter is a user-maintained whitelist which blocks everything except your trusted devices; you administer it usually from your router console under

Wireless Settings or a similarly titled panel. Although a potentially arduous technique, using a MAC filter puts some major obstacles between malicious actors snooping on Wi-Fi and your network.

Unlike one might assume, MAC addresses are not an Apple-specific invention by any means; rather it is a universally embraced technology for all networking devices devised by *Xerox Network Systems*.

- **Become mysterious by concealing your wireless connection.** Many routers offer the option of hiding the name of your wireless network or the *service set identifier (SSID)*. You should enable this feature. At the very least, change your Wi-Fi's default name, as not doing this might inform your potential attackers of the make of your router, facilitating their nefarious activities.

- Some devices allow you to set the broadcasting power of your router, usually donated in percentages. Try dropping that from 100% down to whichever amount still gets picked up by your devices.

- Finally, lock up your routers in secure areas of your home or office to make physical access to them as difficult as possible. Only you and/or your trusted system administrators need to service them.

- **Change your DNS settings.** Like you may know, *Domain Name Service (DNS)* is a protocol which controls the translation of IP addresses, which devices like, into

domain names, which humans tend to prefer
(e.g., www.apress.com). While the default DNS settings
(usually provided by one's *Internet service provider*) work
just fine, there are better alternatives out there. Many
third-party DNS products offer faster data transmission
and added security than their default counterparts; they
often block malicious websites from loading altogether
(see Table 6-2). Changing your DNS is simple and can
be done either in router devices (recommended) or on a
software level within an operating system.

Table 6-2. *Some popular third-party providers of DNS as of Q2 2020*

DNS Provider	IP Addresses (Primary/ Secondary)	Notes
Quad9.net	9.9.9.9, 149.112.112.112	Blocks malicious domains, collects anonymous usage and geolocation data, cooperates with *IBM X-Force* for state-of-the-art threat intelligence
Open DNS	Home: 208.67.222.222, 208.67.220.220 FamilyShield: 208.67.222.222, 208.67.220.220	Claims 100% uptime, *FamilyShield* DNS is preconfigured to block adult content
Google Public DNS	8.8.8.8, 8.8.4.4	Provides global coverage for a fast service to a worldwide clientele, collects user data
Verisign Public DNS	64.6.64.6, 64.6.65.6	Claims no user data is ever sold to 3rd parties

- **Consider investing in a hardware-based firewall for your organization.** While usually overkill for home users, organizations and businesses shouldn't spend a day online without a dedicated hardware firewall. While quite expensive, these units offer a plethora of benefits to software- or router-based solutions. Unlike their software-based brethren, hardware firewalls are online 24/7; they employ more sophisticated forms of traffic analysis and are generally more apt at detecting malicious activities. Configuring a single hardware unit instead of every individual computer running a software firewall saves a lot of time in business settings. Also, larger organizations depending solely on routers for blocking nefarious online elements often end up bottlenecking their data traffic. Many hardware firewalls also come with extensive support for virtual private networks, which are discussed next. This allows secure remote access by trusted employees, for one.

- Popular manufacturers of business-oriented hardware firewall units include *Netgear, Cisco, Juniper, Zyxel*, and *Netgate*.

When configured correctly, the different varieties of firewalls aren't usually mutually exclusive. Even with a hardware firewall guarding your network, you should have a secondary system in place. Popular operating systems all have their built-in software firewalls in 2020. A reliable third-party software-based solution should also do the trick. We'll discuss some of these later in this chapter.

IPv6

IPv4 is slowly being superseded by IPv6, a 128-bit specification with approximately 340 undecillion (i.e., 340 followed by a whopping 36 zeros) unique IP addresses. This should last us a while, unless we somehow colonize numerous other planets in the very near future and the colonists breed on them rather uncontrollably.

IPv6 looks something like this: *09f7:9cd0:0ed0:1538:0000:0000:7360:0090*. Compared to the quaint dot-separated four-octet notation of IPv4, this may seem rather intimidating to us humans. However, we can at least remove all leading zeros from IPv6 addresses, changing our example earlier to *9f7:9cd0:ed0:1538:::7360:90*. That's slightly more memorable.

During 2020, around 25–30% of the Internet was provided in IPv6 (Internet Society, 2020). These numbers are in flux due to the still somewhat maturing technology. Organizations and individuals have been increasingly provided with IPv6 support in both network devices and operating systems since 1998. Dating back to Windows Vista, Microsoft began offering IPv6 support out of the box, while on the Apple side of town, the 2011 release of MacOS 10.7 Lion saw the same for Mac users. Many modern Linux distributions, too, work beautifully with the new protocol.

How soon the new protocol becomes omnipresent is down to providers of online services. So far, some big players, including Google, AT&T, and Facebook, have been involved in promoting the joys of IPv6 to the masses. Thousands of major ISPs and web-based companies vowed to enable IPv6 support permanently on the *World IPv6 Launch Event*, organized by the Internet Society, in June of 2012.

Now, a much larger pool of IP addresses aside, IPv6 offers some other great benefits over IPv4, too.

- **IP Security (IPsec).** This is an important feature and built right into the IPv6 protocol. Although available for

IPv4, data sent using IPsec with this older protocol was sometimes blocked by firewalls, due to malware being capable of piggybacking on these data packets. Not so much with IPv6 IPsec.

- **Speed.** Due to IPv6 not needing any network address translation (NAT), data communications over IPv6 tend to be less congested. As a result, your Internet traffic may feel slightly snappier, at least when using a fully IPv6-compliant Internet service provider (ISP).

- **Facilitating Internet of Things (IoT).** With IPv4, getting IoT devices (e.g., smartphones and wearable gadgets) communicating with each other is sometimes a chore. This is usually attributable to the use of NAT. With IPv6, addressing devices in the IoT realm becomes a more secure and streamlined process.

Virtual Private Network (VPN)

There's a pretty safe way to transmit data even in the virtual wild west of the Internet: this is known as a *virtual private network (VPN)*. A connection secured with this approach is called a *tunnel*. In an ideal situation, no outside actor, be they scammers or governments, can snoop in on VPN traffic. Secure virtual private networks use various varieties of *tunneling protocols* for their encryption. Basically, the transmitted data is repackaged, thus being secured even when sent over public networks. Popular tunneling protocols include the aging, but fast *Point-to-Point Tunneling Protocol (PPTP)* and *OpenVPN*, a modern and robust protocol available for all popular operating systems. The latter is also capable of passing through most firewalls which are sometimes configured to block

VPN access. OpenVPN is open source with a free Community Edition and a paid Access Server version which provides additional features.

In theory VPNs are never a bad idea. There are some issues, however, when it comes to states with less than amazing human rights records spying on their VPN-powered citizens. Many paid providers of these services maintain more or less thorough logs of their users' activities. A government opposed to specific opinions might demand access to these logs disposing of the element of anonymity from the proceedings altogether.

On the whole the benefits of implementing a VPN into your online life outweigh the drawbacks. Even casual browsers benefit from the added security it provides when using public Wi-Fi connections around cafés and other establishments; such unsecured traffic can be eavesdropped on rather trivially. Casual browsers aside, this is also important for both political activists and businesspeople having their morning latte with Wi-Fi. For a less critical purpose, VPNs can be harnessed to sidestep geo-blocking in which a service, such as Netflix, limits geographic regions a user is trying to connect from.

A *kill switch* in the context of virtual private networks refers to an automated process of shutting down a secure tunnel if the system detects a breach or simply malfunctions.

There are numerous VPNs in different configurations available for current-day platforms; see Table 6-3 for a rundown on some of the most popular ones. Usually, more servers at a VPN's disposal translates to better security and/or faster operations overall. Also, what is relevant is the geographic distribution of these servers; a hundred servers in two countries is often less secure than fifty spread all over the world. As you can observe, some VPNs are more rich in features than others.

Table 6-3. *Some popular providers of virtual private networks as of Q2 2020. The pricing presented is an approximation subject to some fluctuation*

Product	Cost	Features
Nord VPN	From 3.50 USD per month for a three-year plan	A promise of a "strict no logging policy," kill switch, secures up to six devices, over 5500 servers
Mullvad VPN	5 USD per month	Easy setup, open source, over 500 servers
Express VPN	7.50 USD per month for a 12-month plan	Over 3000 servers in 94 countries, 24/7 tech support, immune to Google and YouTube, etc. geo-blocking
Hotspot Shield	3 USD per month for a three-year plan	Over 3200 servers, 24/7 tech support

Setting Up a VPN for Windows

Many VPN providers offer their own custom software for setting up a secure network, but that might result in waste of precious disk space and you having less control over your connections. However, you can manually set your VPN up to avoid these issues. Let's start with Windows 10 as our operating system.

- **Access Settings.** Navigate to *Network & Internet.*

- **Select "VPN".** Click *Add a VPN connection.* This will take you to a settings screen.

- **Choose "VPN Provider".** Select the option *Windows (built-in).*

- **Fill in the Connection name.** You should give your VPN connection a title which makes sense, as in it reflects the name of the actual VPN provider (e.g., Nord VPN).

- **Fill in the Server name or address.** These details will be issued by your VPN service. Generally, this is presented in the form of a URL, for example, *apress-is. thebest.com*.

- **Select a VPN protocol.** Out of the several protocols available, pick the one supported by your VPN provider (e.g., *PPTP*).

- Navigate to the drop-down menu labeled **Type of sign-in info**. In most cases you'll be entering your username and password, as issued by your VPN provider, into the associated fields.

- **Click Save.** Go back to Network & Internet settings. Choose your new VPN connection and click *Connect*. You should now be able to go online using a secure virtual private network.

VPN in MacOS

As is the case with Windows, you may want to use manual VPN configuration for your Apple computer(s). For modern versions of MacOS, the process is as follows:

- **Navigate to System Preferences.** You can do this by clicking the Apple logo found on the top-left part of the screen.

- **Select Network.** A new window will appear. Click the plus sign (+) on the bottom-left part of this window.

- **Choose "VPN" from the list of options.** Also select the type of VPN your provider has issued you with.

- **Click Create.** Enter a meaningful and/or memorable service name.

- **Fill in the Server Address.** This can be in the form of a URL or an IP address.

- **Enter your account name**. Your account name is provided by the vendor of the VPN.

- **Click Authentication Settings.** Enter the type of encryption method which your VPN provider supports.

- **Select User Authentication.** Usually you will need to choose the option of *Password*. Follow this up by selecting the type of *Machine Authentication* your VPN provider offers. In many cases it'll be *Shared Secret*. Click *Ok*.

- **Click Advanced.** Tick the checkbox on *Send all traffic over VPN connection* in *Options*.

- **Click Ok, Apply, and Connect.**

VPN in Ubuntu Linux

For Linux, few VPN providers seem to offer custom software bundles with graphical user interfaces. One of the most robust VPN clients/protocols for Linux comes in the form of OpenVPN, as mentioned previously in the chapter. We will next go through the steps for installing an Ubuntu-based VPN using this solution. These steps will be similar for most modern distributions of Linux.

- **Make an account with the VPN provider of your choosing.** They should provide configuration files for Linux on their website (with the file extension of *.ovpn*); for example, Nord VPN offers theirs at `https://nordvpn.com/ovpn`.

- **Download and install Ubuntu OpenVPN packages.** Open a Terminal window and type in the following: *sudo apt-get install network-manager-openvpn-gnome.*

- **Click the NetworkManager icon in Ubuntu.** Navigate to *VPN Off* ➤ *VPN Settings* ➤ *VPN.* Click the plus (+) button next to VPN.

- **Select OpenVPN in the dialog window for Add VPN.** If this option is not visible, restart your computer and try again.

- **Click Import from file.** Navigate to the folder where you downloaded the .ovpn-files into. Double-click these files.

- **A window title Add a VPN will appear prepopulated with server information.** Enter your username and password into the appropriate fields.

- **Navigate back to NetworkManager.** Select the VPN server you wish to connect to.

Safe Emailing with OpenPGP

A secure cryptographic system needs secure communications with the outside world. Touted as "the most widely used email encryption standard," implementations of *OpenPGP* do have a good track record of securing communications in the digital era. OpenPGP is maintained by the *OpenPGP Working Group* of the *Internet Engineering Task Force (IETF)*, an open standards organization founded in 1986. OpenPGP itself was standardized in 1997. Originally, the IETF was supported by the US federal government. Since 1993 the organization has developed standards under the aegis of the Internet Society, which in turn is a global nonprofit organization.

Several implementations of this public-key solution are available for Windows, MacOS, Linux, Android, and iOS. The current OpenPGP specification (i.e., *RFC 4880*) names numerous robust algorithms such as *ElGamal*, *RSA*, and *AES* in several varieties of strength.

OpenPGP technology integrates with mail clients such as *Microsoft Outlook*, *Apple Mail*, or Mozilla's *Thunderbird*. It can also be used in tandem with several popular browsers such as *Firefox* or *Chrome* through add-ons. Table 6-4 lists some easy-to-use OpenPGP implementations which add another layer of security for smaller businesses.

Table 6-4. *Some varieties of OpenPGP implementations as of Q2 2020*

Product	Platform(s)	Cost	URL
Canary Mail	MacOS & iOS	MacOS 20 USD, iOS 10 USD	`www.canarymail.io`
Flowcrypt for Gmail	Extension for *Firefox & Chrome*, app for *Android*	None for limited version, 5 USD a month for advanced version	flowcrypt.com
GPG Suite	MacOS	Free (25 USD for extended support plan for *GPG Mail*)	gpgtools.org
GPG4Win	Windows	Free	`www.gpg4win.de`
Enigmail for Mozilla Thunderbird	MacOS, Windows, Linux	Free	enigmail.net
Pretty Easy Privacy	Windows Outlook extension, Android	20 USD for Outlook (5 devices per license), 3 USD for Android	`www.pep.security.com`

Draft Begone! Securing Windows

In this section, we will review how to build the most secure Windows-based system from the ground up. We'll be focusing on the latest iteration of the operating system, Windows 10, since support for version 7 was phased out in January 2020 and its follow-up Windows 8.1 will be joining it soon enough.

Windows-Security Musts

Encryption aside, you should stick to certain policies when it comes to looking after the security of your devices running the Windows operating system. Let's review these first before proceeding into more cryptographic territory.

- **Download and install every critical/security update offered by Windows Update.** You can access the *Windows Update* in *Settings* under *Update and Security*. Windows is usually more than happy to have you restart your computer after an update to fully install it. Do so, too, without hesitation.

- **Make sure the *Windows Defender Firewall* is enabled.** This feature should be enabled out of the box on Windows 10. To confirm this, navigate to *Control Panel* ➤ *System and Security* ➤ *Windows Defender Firewall*. Click *Turn Windows Defender Firewall on or off*. Whenever this firewall is triggered by suspicious-sounding programs, it's usually best to select *Cancel* in the ensuing prompt.

- **Keep your *Microsoft Defender* running and up to date.** This is a free anti-malware software package shipped with every copy of Windows 10. Although its ability to detect malicious software was modest at first, since 2016 or so it has turned out to be a very useful addition to your security stack providing robust real-time threat scanning. The software also integrates with Microsoft browsers (i.e., *Internet Explorer* and *Microsoft Edge*) and also provides automatic scans of files downloaded with other non-Microsoft browsers. Microsoft Defender was called *Windows Defender* prior to a late 2019 update.

A Bit More on BitLocker

Backdoored or not, Microsoft's BitLocker offers a decent level of encryption for laypeople and smaller businesses with no qualms with the government. Requiring the Pro or Enterprise editions of Windows 10, initiating the encryption process is quite simple. As mentioned in Chapter 3, navigating to *Control Panel* ➤ *System and Security* ➤ *BitLocker Drive Encryption*, one simply clicks *Turn on BitLocker* to start the process (see Figure 6-3).

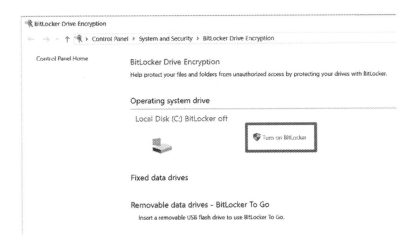

Figure 6-3. *The Windows 10 BitLocker setting*

Please refer to Chapter 4 for a refresher on the basic implementation of BitLocker.

Now, elaborating on more advanced features of BitLocker, we'll get more in depth with some additional security measures on offer such as *Trusted Platform Modules (TPMs)*. Like you may remember, these are types of hardware-based cryptoprocessors which can greatly enhance the security of your system. Often built-in into a computer's motherboard, these devices aren't always switched on by default. Windows 10 manages TPM chips on autopilot, making their manual configuration unnecessary in some cases.

Most computers marketed as *enterprise* or *business class* have built-in TPM-devices out of the box. Cheaper PCs might contain a socket for these devices, but you may have to purchase and install the chip yourself. Some older consumer PCs in particular offer no support for TPMs of any kind. Pay attention to the product specifications.

BIOS, UEFI, and TPM

Not even the latest version of Windows can evoke TPM if it's disabled in a computer's *Basic Input/Output System (BIOS)*. An older approach, a BIOS was built into every PC motherboard and was the first thing executed when you switched the power on. It governed many aspects of a computer's hardware and loaded an operating system, should one exist on connected storage media. This approach often had a charming simplicity to it (see Figure 6-4). BIOS-based computers are still very much around as of 2020.

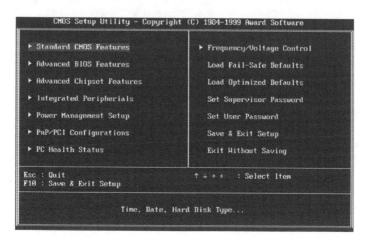

Figure 6-4. A BIOS screen on a typical Windows PC of the late 1990s

In these older systems, you can usually enter BIOS settings by holding down either the delete or F2 key. Navigate to the page mentioning TPM and set it to "enabled".

Now, the closer we got to 2010, the more PC's came out equipped with technology known as *Unified Extensible Firmware Interface (UEFI)*.

Apple made a switch from an *Open Firmware* BIOS equivalent to an implementation of *EFI* when swapping *PowerPC* processors in their products to their Intel-manufactured counterparts. The process took place between late 2005 and early 2006. As of 2020 all new Macs still use Intel CPUs.

A replacement for BIOS, a UEFI served the same purpose but offered more features, improved boot-up speed, and additional security features. For one, a UEFI-equipped computer is immune against many of the threats BIOS had as a feature called *secure boot* mitigates a lot of them. However, a UEFI makes installation of other operating systems than what a computer came shipped with a tad inconvenient. Still, if given a choice of either an older, BIOS-equipped PC or one with UEFI, the latter is a far better bet from a security standpoint. Again, you should make sure your UEFI-equipped computer has its TPM setting on "enabled" at all times; it may or may not default to this setting out of the box.

TPM 1.2 vs. 2.0

There are two important revisions of TPM technology: versions 1.2 and 2.0. The former only supports the RSA algorithm with the SHA-1 hashing technique. Many industry professionals are therefore steering clear from TPM version 1.0 due to these limitations; it's recommended you do too. For one, version 2.0 has support for the mighty AES up to its most robust 256-bit variety. It also supports such hashing algorithms as SHA-384,

SHA-512, and even the most rugged varieties of the SHA-3 family. Using TPM 2.0 simply makes sense. However, not all TPM-devices are built equal and the algorithms they support may vary. Again, read the specs before investing in a computer.

A Fresh Start: Resetting a TPM

Some scenarios exist which justify resetting a TPM-device (i.e., deleting the passwords contained within one). The strongest case for this is when one is reinstalling the operating system. On occasion *Windows Defender* might prompt you to clear the TPM as well. Remember, Windows 10 will automatically take control of the cleared TPM once reinstalled and fill it with data that needs to be there. Before resetting a TPM-device, make sure you have backups of your passwords and other related information; it can't be retrieved after a reset.

This process is quite simple for Windows 10. Navigate to *Settings* ➤ *Update & Security* ➤ *Windows Security* ➤ *Device security*. Click *Security Processor Details*. Next, select *Security Device Troubleshooting*. Finally, click *Clear TPM*. You'll be asked to restart the computer. Do so, and Windows will rebuild the data on your TPM on its next launch.

You might have the option of using non-Microsoft drivers for your TPM. This might prove to be an issue at some point; it's best to stick with certified Windows-based drivers. Also, with Windows 10 it's better to not utilize any TPM-clearing function found in the UEFI interface. Rather, let the operating system take care of that.

A Nice, Ripe Stick of USB, Please

Like discussed in Chapter 4, BitLocker can be configured to utilize a USB-stick in case a TPM isn't available – and even when it is. This is a fine additional countermeasure against malicious actors not in possession of said stick and one that's easy to implement. In BitLocker parlance, this is known as the *USB Key Mode*, and as previously mentioned, it can be combined with a password, a TPM, or both. While the option for relying solely on a USB device is available, this is not a recommended approach. Have you ever lost a memory-stick or two? That's why. Again, whenever feasible, secure your BitLocker equipped with every means available.

Utilizing a USB device in conjunction with BitLocker requires a computer with a BIOS/UEFI which supports booting up from USB. These days that is pretty much the norm. Your mileage with older computers may vary significantly.

Minding Your MacOS

Moving on to the Apple ecosystem, you should be aware that all varieties of MacOS since version 10.7 (Lion) come built-in with a great encryption solution in the form of *FileVault 2*. As with other closed-source solution, it may or may not come with corporate/government backdoors. As a Mac user, your best bet is to at least enhance your system's security by applying a second layer of encryption in the form of file containers. For this, the 100% open source *VeraCrypt* is probably your best choice; like *FileVault 2* it supports all versions of MacOS since version 10.7. There are other choices for your MacOS-related cryptographic solutions. We'll go in depth with these soon. But first, let's review some basic security measures every Mac user should be aware of at all times.

MacOS-Security Musts

Whether you are an individual or in charge of an organization, there are certain policies related to security you should always implement. Needless to say, these approaches should have the scope of every single computer under your roof.

- **Install updates without delay.** When you get the prompt to update, do it immediately. Updates aren't just a bunch of pretty new emoticons; an unpatched, vulnerable system can be potentially compromised in seconds. Also, restart your Mac to complete the installation process without delay.

- **Enable the MacOS application firewall.** This feature is usually not switched on by default. Navigate to *System Preferences* ➤ *Security & Privacy* ➤ *Firewall*. Click the lock in the bottom left of the window and enter your system password. Proceed to click *Enable Firewall*. You should also click *Firewall Options* and tick the box next to *Enable Stealth Mode* to make your system slightly harder to find for the numerous malicious actors out there. This setting won't make a world of a difference if you are behind a firewalled router but it can't hurt.

- **Limit sharing.** Your Mac is willing to communicate with the outside world through numerous avenues. From a security point of view, it's a wise move to limit these communications to a bare minimum. Visit *System Preferences* ➤ *Sharing* and you'll get to choose which forms of data your computer gets to share (see Figure 6-5). Under many scenarios, you can simply untick all of the boxes; of most critical scrutiny should be *Remote Management* and *Remote Login*.

Figure 6-5. *The MacOS sharing settings screen*

- **Review your Gatekeeper settings.** Since MacOS 10.7
  (Lion), Apple has included a security feature called
  Gatekeeper in its operating systems. This is a relatively
  solid tool for blocking many varieties of malicious
  software from executing on one's system. Now, as of
  MacOS 10.12 (Sierra), there are only two settings for
  Gatekeeper: either allowing the execution of software
  downloaded from the Apple App Store or both from
  the App Store and (Apple) Identified Developers.
  For maximum security it's a good idea to only trust
  software which originates from the App Store. If you're
  on a Mac with an older operating system (e.g., MacOS
  10.11 "El Capitan" or earlier), you will also see a third
  Gatekeeper option: allow apps downloaded from
  anywhere. You should never enable this setting. To
  review your Gatekeeper settings, navigate to *System
  Preferences* ➤ *Security & Privacy* ➤ *General.*

- **Create a nonadministrator account for trivial use.**
  Administrators are great and necessary people, but an
  administrator's account falling into the wrong hands
  can be a disaster. Therefore, it makes sense to have a
  secondary account without administrator privileges.
  For this, you should navigate to *Users & Groups* in your
  Mac's *System Preferences*. Also, make sure to disable
  automatic login from *Login Options* (see Figure 6-6).

Figure 6-6. *The MacOS user settings screen. Note Login Options in
the bottom left*

T2, Judgment Chip: TPM, Apple Style

With the release of the mighty 2017 *iMac Pro*, Apple has been including
a hybrid TPM/accelerator chip in many of their computers. The *T2
chip* is Apple's second-generation custom microchip used for on-
the-fly encryption and several other purposes. Its functions include

dedicated audio management, webcam-related image processing, and cryptographic functions for one's solid-state drive(s). The T2 runs on a discrete operating system known as *BridgeOS* with which the average user rarely needs to tamper with. Having a T2 in your Mac not only makes it more secure, but also slightly faster as quite a number of tasks are offloaded from the CPU onto this chip. The only downside is it's pretty much impossible to recover data from a Mac with a failed T2 chip as the system is quite impenetrable.

All T2-equipped Macs are issued a *Mac Unique ID (UID)* and a *Device Group ID (GID)* during manufacturing. Both the UID and GID are tied to a particular device only. These strings are inaccessible by any software or hardware outside of their environment, which Apple calls the *Secure Enclave*. The *UID* and *GID* are used by the cryptographic engine in a T2 device. To the outside world, this engine shows only the results of its encryption or decryption operations. Not even Apple or their suppliers can later access the UID contents directly. This is the first layer of security in a T2 chip.

Now, when FileVault is enabled in MacOS, your SSD-drives are quite safe from prying eyes combined with Apple's custom chip. The T2 chip's cryptographic functions operate under FileVault using the rock-solid AES-256 algorithm using the XTS operating mode as discussed in Chapter 4. As the encryption/decryption process is also completely offloaded onto Apple's custom chip, there is no longer any additional speed penalty to any of your solid-state disks. Even when FileVault is disabled on a T2-equipped Mac, the SSDs in the system remain encrypted. However, they are then only protected by the hardware UID. As all the drives are subjected to encryption in every case, switching FileVault on later isn't a time-consuming process and is highly recommended for the extra layer of security it provides.

As of Q2 2020, the following Apple computers come with the T2 chip onboard:

- Desktops: iMac Pro (2017), Mac Mini (2018), Mac Pro (2019), and presumably later models

- Laptops: MacBook Air (2018), MacBook Pro (2018), and later models

---

Not sure if a particular Mac has the T2 chip or just feel like perusing some information concerning one? Open *About this Mac* and click *System Report*. Select the *Hardware* tab. If it has a subtab called *Controller* also mentioning the chip, you're in luck.

T2 Maintenance 101

As with traditional TPM modules, issues may turn up which might require you to refresh your T2 chip settings. Apple has integrated its *System Management Controller (SMC)* within the T2; therefore, if your computer has sudden issues with its cooling fans, external ports, or power management, a reset of the SMC might be in order. We'll now review the procedure for newer T2-equipped Macs.

For your Apple desktop, first shut your computer down. Disconnect its power lead for 15 seconds. After this reconnect the power lead and wait for five seconds. Finally, press the power button like you normally would to start up your Mac.

As for T2-equipped Apple laptops, the process to reset the chip is a tad more complex. First, shut down your MacBook. Then press and hold the *right Shift*, *left Option*, and *left Control* keys for at least seven seconds. Continue by holding those keys while you also press and hold the power button for yet another seven seconds. Now, release the keys and the power button, wait for a couple of seconds, and finally just power up the laptop.

Security Software for Mac

We'll now review some more security solutions for your MacOS-based environments.

- **AppCrypt by Cisdem** (30/45 USD for a lifetime home/ business license)

  A tool catered perfectly not just for worried parents but also for the organizational clientele, *AppCrypt* works to block specific websites. Bid farewell to your employees wasting time on *Facebook* and *Twitter* with this Mac-specific solution. In addition to websites, you also get to prohibit the use of specific applications you're not particularly fond of, such as games and other time-consumers, with the use of a master password only you should be aware of. AppCrypt makes it somewhat hard to circumvent its blocking prowess by forcing said master password on MacOS *System Preferences*, *Terminal*, *Activity Monitor*, and *Console*.

  AppCrypt has scheduling functionality, so you can set the exact date and time to lift your app usage bans. This feature won't work for website blocking, however. AppCrypt is available for MacOS versions 10.10 (Yosemite) or newer.

- Discover AppCrypt here and download a demo version: www.cisdem.com/appcrypt-mac.html.

- **Encrypto by MacPaw**

  Sometimes just a few of your files need that extra layer of security. *Encrypto* is a nifty and free solution for securing your individual files and folders on the MacOS. Relying on the 256-bit variety of AES, it offers without a doubt robust cryptographic capabilities. Not only that, you can share your encrypted files with Windows users, as Encrypto is also available for Microsoft's range of operating systems starting from *Windows XP*. On a Mac the software also allows for easy integration into your OS with an additional Share button that's there for sending your files over to *iMessages* or *AirDrop*. Support for decrypting .crypt-files in iOS devices is lacking as of early 2020.

The program features a clean, user-friendly graphical user interface so no typing into terminal windows is needed to create a very secure file container with a .crypto extension. By simply dragging and dropping a file into the program window and entering a password is all it takes.

With Encrypto you can also add handy password hints into each file should you choose to; these may be especially handy when sharing data. There is the minor annoyance of a window requesting you share "anonymous user data," whatever that means, every time you shut *Encrypto* down. However, this shouldn't dissuade you from trying out this fine piece of cryptographic software.

- Download Encrypto here: `https://macpaw.com/encrypto`.

Staying Safer in Linux

Now it's time to take a deeper look into the Linux side of things. Although we took a glance at a few cryptographic solutions for this great operating system in Chapter 3, it's time to review a couple more popular pieces of security software for this fine operating system.

CryFS

Offering pretty much a complete cryptographic solution, *CryFS* is a wonderful piece of open source software for most distributions of Linux. Not only does it protect local data on your computer, but it can also be harnessed for cloud-based services, such as *DropBox*. CryFS makes sure only encrypted data leaves your system. This encompasses not only your files and directories, but metadata (including file size information) as well.

The encryption approach in CryFS actually consists of a double-layer process. First, it uses the most robust algorithm we currently have, the AES-256, for an external layer. After this the user can choose to implement a different encryption scheme for an inner layer. Both of these layers share the password given by the user. A truly unique solution, CryFS is highly recommended for more advanced cryptographers looking for the current state of the art in Linux security.

Let's now go through the basic steps of getting CryFS running on your Linux distribution, shall we?

1. **Installation of CryFS for Ubuntu and Debian is simple.** Just enter the following into a terminal window: *$ sudo apt install cryfs*

2. **Next we create two new directories with CryFS.** Type in the following: *$ cryfs realdir virtdir*. You can naturally choose whatever names you want for both of these. The latter (i.e., *virtdir* in our example) is

the name for a virtual, encrypted directory which is managed in the background by the CryFS system. The program will ask for specific settings when making these directories; it's okay to go with the defaults.

3. **You can now operate with this CryFS virtual directory to store, modify, and delete any data you wish in a very secure environment.** Simply use the cd command to enter the encrypted portion by typing *$ cd virtdir*. The actual data will be stored and encrypted by CryFS in the first directory we specified (i.e., *realdir*) at all times.

4. **Unmounting an encrypted CryFS partition is simple.** Just enter *$ cryfs-unmount virtdir* (or whichever name you chose for the virtual directory).

- Discover CryFS here: `www.cryfs.org`.

CryFS is also available for Windows. However, this version is only supported to an experimental degree. See the project website for installation instructions and proceed with caution; it's best to use other Windows-based cryptographic solutions as of Q2 2020.

FireStarter

Nearly all Linux distributions come with *iptables*, a piece of software which functions as a firewall. Being a command-line utility, it can be hard to grasp by beginners and can actually cause major issues with security and connectivity if poorly configured. Luckily graphical user interfaces for this vital part of Linux security do exist. One of the more established ones is *FireStarter*, a free and intuitive firewall interface which works great for the less experienced users.

Although the latest stable release of FireStarter dates back to 2005, it's still a solid addition to your Linux experience. Setting the program up is easy by running a three-step wizard. You get some great functionality with FireStarter, such as detailed logs and easy rule-making for all of your online traffic-control needs.

- Download FireStarter here: `http://sourceforge.net/projects/firestarter`.

You vs. Malware

As discussed previously, nothing can cripple even the most well-encrypted system faster than a dose of potent malware. We'll now delve into this issue in detail, presenting some of the best solutions against even the most ingenious varieties of malicious software in Windows-, MacOS-, or Linux-based environments.

Contrary to a somewhat popular belief, there are in fact a plethora of well-established free anti-malware software suites for your immediate download. We'll now go more in depth with some of these solutions. However, corporations and smaller organizations love their commercial anti-malware licenses. And this is for a reason; these usually provide better support, features, and in some cases, less strain on one's hardware. We'll also explore the world of paid security software, focusing only on solutions with the best features and minimal hits on performance.

Avast Antivirus by Avast

One of the most popular anti-malware solutions on the market, Avast products are available for Windows, MacOS, Linux, Android, and iOS. Their free antivirus tool provides solid protection against malware of all types as well as scanning for threats on Wi-Fi. The only downside in the suite is the inclusion of a touch of advertisement.

While individuals can gain much peace of mind from Avast's free tools, the company offers even more value to corporations and organizations. For one, *Avast Business Antivirus Pro* offers great additional features such as secure file shredding and real-time data protection for teams working in Microsoft's SharePoint environment (see Table 6-5).

Table 6-5. *The available varieties of Avast solutions for businesses in Q2 2020. The pricing presented is an approximation subject to some fluctuation*

License	Cost Per Annum Per Computer	Main Selling Points
Antivirus	30 USD	Automatic signature updates, Avast Firewall, CyberCapture file analysis of suspicious programs
Antivirus Pro	40 USD	Secure file shredder, Microsoft SharePoint and Exchange (email) security
Antivirus Pro Plus	50 USD	Webcam protection, additional password security

The Avast story is not without controversy. In January 2020 it was revealed that the company may have sold thousands of its users' profiles for commercial gain. Avast made a statement claiming the data was not enough to identify any users and apparently dropped the practice entirely.

- Download Avast Antivirus for free: www.avast.com.

Avira Antivirus by Avira Operations GmbH & Co

With its roots in 1986 Germany, Avira is a long-standing antiviral product of a very high caliber. Some coming in both free and paid versions, Avira offerings are a sturdy, well-received line of products available for multiple platforms. Unfortunately, support for Linux was dropped in 2013.

Avira claims their anti-malware software is among the most lightweight (i.e., easiest on a device's hardware). In addition, their offerings have received numerous awards in several categories over the years. The company also insists that they are unwilling to sell your information to any third parties. To their credit Germany does have a good recent track record of protecting the privacy of its citizens and the users of information systems in general. This is in part due to historical reasons.

A *zero-day vulnerability* is a flaw in any piece of software which may or may not be known to its creators but remains unfixed for the time being. Usually, this is due to time constraints and will be addressed more or less swiftly in the form of an update. However, malicious actors can cause a lot of damage to the users of software with these types of vulnerabilities.

Avira Free Antivirus is a popular anti-malware solution for Windows, MacOS, Android, and iOS. Its commercial counterpart especially, the *Avira Antivirus Pro*, remains a constant favorite among reviewers and users alike. Avira offers many excellent solutions suited for both individuals and organizations (see Table 6-6).

Table 6-6. *The available main varieties of Avira products in Q2 2020.*
The pricing presented is an approximation subject to some fluctuation

Solution	Cost Per Annum	Main Selling Points
Free Antivirus	n/a	Robust protection against most types of malware and malicious websites
Antivirus Pro	40 USD	Customer support, email attachment, and USB-device scanning, ad-free
Free Security Suite	n/a	Includes free antivirus, system speedup, VPN (500 MB/month), Software Updater, and seven other programs
Internet Security Suite	50 USD	Automatic software updates, advanced ransomware protection, customer support
Avira Prime	115 USD	Computer speed optimization components, support for up to five devices, premium apps for iOS and Android
Antivirus Pro Business Edition	30 USD	Avira Protection Cloud, AI-based zero-day vulnerability –protection, ransomware protection
Antivirus for Endpoint	120 USD	File server protection, content filtering policies
Antivirus for Small Business	180 USD	Additional email security, email receiver protection, Microsoft Exchange security

- Download Avira Antivirus for free: `www.avira.com`.

Bitdefender Antivirus

In charge of a vast variety of high-quality products for a multitude of systems, Bitdefender is a company with great credentials in computer security solutions. Free products notwithstanding (including their *Virus Scanner for Mac* found on *Apple App Store*), Bitdefender has to offer some powerful paid suites for most of your online security needs (see Table 6-7).

Table 6-7. *The main varieties of Bitdefender products in Q2 2020. The pricing presented is an approximation subject to some fluctuation*

Product	Cost (Per First Year)	Platform	Main Selling Points
Antivirus Plus 2020	30 USD for 3 computers	Windows	Multilayer ransomware protection
Internet Security 2020	40 USD for 3 computers	Windows	Parental controls
Total Security 2020	45 USD for 5 computers	Windows, MacOS, iOS, Android	Support for three additional platforms, operating system-optimization tools

- Explore Bitdefender's range of products here: www.bitdefender.com.

SpyBot – Search and Destroy by Safer-Networking Ltd

Bursting to the scene all the way back in 1999, *SpyBot* is a popular and effective countermeasure against malicious software of most varieties for Microsoft Windows operating systems. In addition to its anti-malware tools, the software offers fine anti-rootkit capabilities. The latter come in two varieties, namely, "quick scan" and "deep scan." Like its name states, the former is a fast but somewhat limited type of system analysis. The latter, while more robust, can take anything between half an hour to several hours per your average computer as SpyBot scours hard drives and Windows registries rather vigorously. Unfortunately, the program can occasionally prompt you with more false alarms (i.e., harmless software is appearing as something malicious) than other anti-malware software.

Other functionality offered by SpyBot includes "immunization," a type of preemptive measure against specific vulnerabilities found in Windows and in some of its most popular Internet browsers (e.g., Internet Explorer, Firefox, and Opera). This feature simply blocks your system's access to known malicious websites. Immunizing Windows with SpyBot usually takes only a few seconds and is highly recommended.

SpyBot does take a chunk of a system's resources (i.e., memory) but is free to download and offers much even in this free version. However, real-time protection is only available via a paid license (see Table 6-8). But even if you're feeling stingy and go for the free version, this software will probably become quite dear to you and your Windows-based systems.

Table 6-8. *The available varieties of SpyBot – Search and Destroy in Q2 2020. The pricing presented is an approximation subject to some fluctuation*

License	Cost Per Annum	Main Selling Points
Free	n/a	Anti-spyware, system immunization, rootkit scan
Home	15 USD	Automatic signature updates
Professional	25 USD	Secure file shredder, system registry repair, command-line tools
Corporate	35 USD per device	Customized feature set according to the needs of the business
Technician	55 USD	FileAlyzer file analysis including hex data viewing and editing capabilities

- Download SpyBot – Search and Destroy for free: `www.safer-networking.org/products`.

TDSS Killer and Virus Removal Tool 2015 by Kaspersky Lab

Founded in 1997 in Moscow, *Kaspersky Lab* is a well-respected actor in the business of anti-malware software solutions. Just to be on the safe side, the *US Department of Homeland Security* banned the use of Kaspersky products in all US government departments as of 2017. This move is likely to have been an overreaction as Kaspersky products consistently score very well in many independent security experts' tests.

Not only limited to ta single variety of rootkits, the *TDSSKiller* tool can detect and quarantine other types of malicious software including *ZeroAccess*, *Whistler*, and *RLoader*. As of Q2 2020, the software is supported, updated, and highly recommended. Kaspersky also offers a free general-purpose malware scanner. Unlike its name might state, *Virus Removal Tool 2015* still gets fairly frequent updates as of 2020. Both of these tools are only available for Windows-based systems.

- Download TDSS Killer for free: `https://usa.kaspersky.com/downloads/tdsskiller`.

- Download Virus Removal Tool 2015 for free: `https://support.kaspersky.com/8527`.

TDSS, also known as *Alurion*, was the second most active rootkit in the world in 2010. The program did/does its best to disable all anti-malware solutions on a system and gather sensitive data such as credit card numbers and online credentials.

Stinger by McAfee

A fine addition to your anti-malware arsenal coming in at exactly zero dollars, *Stinger* offers real-time protection in addition to its frequently updated signatures. The program is available for users of both 32- and 64-bit Windows operating systems and does not need any kind of license from McAfee to download or execute. Again, the main lure in Stinger is in the real-time protection. McAfee does state this portion of the software is still in beta testing as of 2020 Q2, but it seems to do its job rather well already. While you shouldn't rely on Stinger alone for your anti-malware needs, it's still a good addition to have in your arsenal.

- Download Stinger for free: `www.mcafee.com/enterprise/en-us/downloads/free-tools/stinger.html`.

In Closing

After finishing this chapter, you will have learned the following:

- What BIOS and UEFI refer to and how they differ

- The best practices for securing a modern operating system

- How to implement proper router security policies, including Wi-Fi security

- How *virtual private networks (VPNs)* benefit you and your organization

- Which anti-malware software suites are out there for Windows, Linux, and MacOS in 2020

In the next chapter we'll be taking a breather from the technical side of things and explore the many fascinating legal aspects surrounding cryptography. For one, did you know being in possession of any type of encrypted material in select countries may in itself constitute a crime? Read all about it in Chapter 7!

References

Internet Society (2020): Measurement activities of IPv6 deployment. Retrieved from: `www.worldipv6launch.org/measurements`

CHAPTER 7

Prohibitions and Legal Issues

As exciting as cryptography can be, dabbling in it may also come with a few rather unpleasant unforeseen legal ramifications – when dealing with certain jurisdictions, that is. We'll now take a gander at digital encryption technology from the sometimes overlooked legal point of view. Starting from the vast landmass called America, we'll have covered most the world's cryptographic restrictions by the end of this chapter. Also, the related matter of various categories of US privacy legislation are explored.

Cryptography is a hot topic; it's a magnificent tool for both congenial and malicious actors in the world. As you deepen your knowledge on the subject, you're bound to run into some landmark court cases – and the associated legal terms. Should you need to brush up on your legalese, a primer is to be found at the end of this chapter, for your convenience.

Note   This chapter is not intended to provide legal advice. Please consult an attorney if you need clarification on any variety of legal information.

© Robert Ciesla 2020
R. Ciesla, *Encryption for Organizations and Individuals*,
https://doi.org/10.1007/978-1-4842-6056-2_7

Missiles, Tanks, and Encryption

Now, until 1992, the export of cryptographic technologies out of the United States was strictly controlled. This type of technology was, after all, considered "auxiliary military equipment" by the Federal Government back in the day. Over the years these restrictions have gradually been relaxed, the main reasons being the Internet, the massive growth of digital commerce – and the first amendment.

Not surprisingly, the legality of digital cryptography was tested in the courts by a couple of landmark cases. Perhaps the most relevant case in the matter, *Bernstein v. United States* took place in 1995, when computers were mostly light gray boxes and the very first *Toy Story* wowed us all. *Daniel J. Berkley* was a strapping young doctoral student at the University of California, Berkeley, with a keen interest in cryptography. He devised his own software-based encryption system, *Snuffle*, and quickly found himself at odds with the Federal Government. Remember, source code of encryption software was still military equipment at the time, listed on the *US Munitions List* alongside ballistic missiles and tanks. Bernstein was aware of this and contacted the State Department. He was told to either register as an arms dealer or forget about it.

With the help of *Electronic Frontier Foundation*, a nonprofit digital rights group, Bernstein appealed on constitutional grounds, and won. President Bill Clinton signed Executive Order 13026 in 1996, which transferred commercial encryption technology from the US Munitions List to the Commerce Control List. And so began a new era of loosening US export regulations on cryptographic systems.

EU's General Data Protection Regulation (GDPR)

Enforced since May of 2018, the *General Data Protection Regulation* changed the way businesses handle their customers' data. The GDPR was created to offer EU citizens greater control over their information whether they are sharing it within or outside of the EU. Businesses not happy to comply with these new regulations face fines up to 20 million EUR.

The GDPR grants eight rights for digital customers.

1. **The right to access.** Individuals have the right to request access to their personal data and to ask how their data is used by a company.

2. **The right to be forgotten.** Whenever consumers stop being customers or if they withdraw their consent, they have the right to have their data deleted.

3. **The right to data portability.** Individuals have a right to transfer their data from one service provider to another.

4. **The right to be informed.** Consumers have to opt in for their data to be gathered and consent must be freely given rather than implied.

5. **The right to have information corrected.** Individuals can have their data updated if it is out of date or incorrect.

6. **The right to restrict processing.** Individuals can request that their data is not used for processing.

7. **The right to object.** This includes the right of individuals to stop the processing of their data for marketing purposes. There are no exemptions to this rule.

8. **The right to be notified.** In case of a data breach, an individual has a right to be informed about this within 72 hours.

The regulation applies to all businesses and organizations established in the EU whether their data is processed inside or outside of this region. A business offering goods and services to EU citizens is also subject to the GDPR. From a consumer's viewpoint, the regulation is certainly very visible as those cookie-related confirmation dialogs on almost every commercial website.

Businesses have criticized the GDPR for its stiff penalties for failure to comply and a strict time frame for implementing these policies.

Cryptography in the United States

Although the United States is quite at ease with encryption in the current year, some restrictions naturally apply. These include exporting this type of technology to the so-called rogue states (sometimes referred to as "states of concern" instead) which in 2019 include Sudan, Venezuela, North Korea, and Iran. Several nations, including Libya, Yugoslavia, and Cuba, have been scrubbed off this list over the years as the political climate changes. The situation is subject to change.

Custom cryptographic software, cryptographic consulting services, and militarized encryption equipment all require an export license. Encryption tools specifically designed, developed, or adapted for military use remain on the tightly controlled US Munitions List.

Encrypted and Crossing the Border

The Fourth Amendment to the US Constitution was created to protect against unreasonable searches and seizures. This doesn't apply to the US border or her airports, however. In *United States v. Arnold (2008)*, the US Ninth Court of Appeals ruled that data on a traveler's electronic materials, including personal files on a laptop computer, may be perused entirely at random. This has caused concern among supporters of the Fourth Amendment as well as professionals who deal with mission-critical data, such as lawyers and scientists.

US Customs and Border Protection (CBP) agents do not require "reasonable suspicion," a legal standard of proof in the United States, to stop and search travelers. He or she may be coerced into revealing passwords by being subjected to lengthy periods of detainment. In addition, CBP and other authorities may confiscate your devices and ship them out for "technical assistance"; there is technology out there in seedy government laboratories which might be able to crack your passwords, no matter how strong. You may or may not see your devices again in this scenario.

The best way of passing through the US border smoothly is to prepare to hand over your key codes. It's therefore best to travel with as little personal or encrypted data as possible. Log out of all cloud services on all of your devices before crossing the border. Either delete your critical data beforehand or, even better, bring blank devices with you with only the minimum of apps needed for your stay. Keep those volatile trade secrets and patent ideas at the office. Any embarrassing mankini and/or swimsuit shots belong at home.

Key Disclosure Laws in the United States

The so-called key disclosure laws refer to legislation which compels an individual to hand over passwords of their digital storage devices to law enforcement. These laws are used to gather evidence to be used in a court of law or for the purposes of national security; they vary greatly between countries.

The Fifth Amendment to the US Constitution protects an individual from self-incrimination. There are no de facto key disclosure laws active in the United States. Some interesting case law on the subject exists, however.

John Doe, a Floridian under investigation in 2012, refused to reveal the passwords to his encrypted devices and was jailed for contempt of court. In *United States v. Doe*, the Eleventh Circuit Court of Appeals held that handing out the password for encrypted data or revealing the decrypted data itself is an act of self-incrimination, so an individual can't be forced to do so by the government.

In *United States v. Kirschner* in 2010, the US District Court for the Eastern District of Michigan held that coercing an individual into revealing a password, even as a response to a grand jury subpoena, constitutes a violation of the Fifth Amendment. Plead the fifth, people.

Key Disclosure Laws in Canada, Europe, and Oceania

Many countries do not share America's mostly reasonable take on key disclosure, although in the Czech Republic, Poland, Iceland, Germany, Sweden, and Switzerland no key disclosure laws are in effect as of 2019. However, de facto punishments for failing to disclose keys, such as detainment and isolation, might apply.

In the Bahamas, law enforcement officers presenting a warrant are entitled to require any person in possession of decryption information (i.e., passwords) to grant access to such decryption information "as it necessary to decrypt data." The penalty for not complying consists of up to a three-year jail sentence and/or a fine of up to 10,000 Bahamian dollars, which is roughly the same amount in US dollars.

The *Canadian Charter of Rights and Freedoms* is applied to every individual, citizen or not, inside the Canadian border, as established in 1985 by the Supreme Court of Canada. The charter protects all people against self-incrimination, including in cases where encrypted devices are a part of an investigation. A decision of the *Quebec Court of Appeal* in 2010, *R. c. Boudreau-Fontaine*, fortified Canada's position on the matter; nobody inside Canada can be punished for not divulging the keys to their devices. However, some dissenting voices have emerged over the years. In 2016, the *Canadian Association of Chiefs of Police (CACP)* proposed new powers that would require suspects to hand over their encryption keys when under criminal investigation. Still, as of 2019 Canada remains faithful to their charter.

In the United Kingdom, a person is required to decrypt data and/or supply passwords to the government without a court order. Failure to do so carries a maximum penalty of two years in jail or five years in the cases of national security or child indecency. Legislation for this practice was introduced in the *Regulation of Investigatory Powers Act (RIPA)*, which came into effect in 2007. Several convictions have been made under this law in recent years.

In Ireland, the police (i.e., the Garda) have the right to demand passwords to encrypted systems in cases of criminal investigation. However, it only applies to a "person at the place which is being searched" or where a person has certain material in their "possession or control."

In the Netherlands, Denmark, Finland, and Belgium, systems administrators and other related personnel are compelled to provide passwords to encrypted systems, should they be in possession of this information. Failure to do say results in fines and in some cases jail. The suspects themselves are not required by law to divulge any keys in any of the above countries.

The *Council of Europe* has influenced the key disclosure debate in Sweden by adopting a convention of forced disclosure. Although no such laws exist yet in 2019 in Sweden, it's quite likely they will be introduced into the country's legislation in the near future.

In Australia the police will, with a magistrate's order, use their wide-ranging power to require "a specified person to provide any information or assistance that is reasonable and necessary to allow the officer to" access computer data that is "evidential material." In practice this means the police have the right to decrypt your devices. Failure to do so might result in a six-month jail sentence.

Although New Zealand doesn't have key disclosure laws per se, the charter may be a tad obscure on the matter. The *Search and Surveillance Act of 2012* states both "The search power cannot be used to require the specified person give any information tending to incriminate them" and "this does not prevent a person exercising a search power from requiring the specified person to provide information." Should a person decline offering his or her decryption keys, there's potentially a three-month jail sentence to look forward to. Also, there has been a push by some elements of New Zealand's government to issue limitless powers to access encrypted devices of citizens, but this policy hasn't manifested so far, as of 2019.

Key Disclosure Laws in Africa

Aside from North Africa, most nations on the continent do not have specific laws for the regulation of encryption. Some exceptions, however, are to be found. In Nigeria, law enforcement is allowed to "use any technology to decode or decrypt any coded or encrypted data contained in a computer into readable text or comprehensible format," as long as a warrant is in effect. Willfully obstructing any law enforcement officer or failing to comply with any lawful inquiry or requests made by any law enforcement agency is a criminal offense. This could be interpreted as including a request to assist in data decryption. Refusing to cooperate is punishable by imprisonment for up to two years, and/or a fine of up to 500,000 NGN which is roughly 1400 USD.

Mozambique's *Code of Criminal Procedure* simply states that encrypted documents must be subject to review by experts in order to decrypt them. This may or may not include a cryptography enthusiast spilling the beans in the form of his or her passwords.

In Angola, the *Law on Combating Crime in the Field of Information and Communication Technologies and Information Society Services* provides that if it becomes necessary for the production of evidence to obtain specific data stored in a particular information system, the "Competent Authority" may order those who have control of such data to provide that data or access to the information system where it is stored under penalty of punishment for qualified disobedience. These orders cannot be directed toward a suspect or a defendant in the proceedings.

World's Toughest Key Disclosure Laws

A few countries are extremely strict when it comes to key disclosure. The judges of France sentence you to jail for three years if you fail to give out your passwords during an investigation. In addition, you're required to pay a fine of 45,000 euros (or roughly 51,000 USD as of 2019). If the suspect's compliance would've prevented a crime, jail time increases to five years and the fine goes up to 75,000 euros (or 85,000 USD).

In India, the central or state governments may order any agency to compel any "subscriber or intermediary or any person in charge of the computer resource" to "extend all facilities and technical assistance" necessary to decrypt information. The penalty for noncompliance is up to seven years of jail and/or a fine.

In South Africa, failure to hand over your password might result in a whopping ten-year jail sentence or a fine of up to two million South African rand, a hefty sum of roughly $145,000. However, a judge must first issue a "decryption direction," a type of warrant, to the person believed to be in possession of the key.

Zimbabwe's *Interception of Communications Act* allows law enforcement agencies to impose "disclosure requirements" to persons in respect of encrypted information where they believe that a key to encrypted information is in the possession of that person, and that a disclosure requirement is necessary for "the interests of national security, to prevent or detect a serious criminal offense, or in the interests of the country's economic wellbeing." They must also believe that the requirement is proportionate to what is being sought. Noncompliance with the disclosure agreement may result in a jail sentence of up to five years, and/or a fine.

Criticism and Blowback

Key disclosure laws have been met with much criticism by numerous pertinent privacy organizations worldwide. Self-incrimination issues aside, the application process of these laws may overlook scenarios where the key has genuinely been lost, forgotten, or subjected to expiration.

Various technological solutions have been used to circumvent key disclosure entirely. These include *deniable encryption*, where a collection of data contains several encrypted portions with separate keys, and *steganography*, where the critical data is hidden in plain sight inside noncritical data. Of course, severe violations to the well-being of a person, such as physical torture, could work to undermine even the aforementioned practices.

A rather ineffective solution, *key escrowing*, has been offered by some government agencies, including the *US Department of Commerce*. An escrow is a system where a third party maintains custody of an item, taking action with it only when a specified condition has been fulfilled between the other two parties involved. A key escrow would be a database containing potentially tens of millions of passwords, or more, handed over to a third party. Governments could only access the database in the case of serious crime investigations. This arrangement would be far from ideal. Issues, such as government employees' ability to abuse access to this database, persist. Naturally, these keys would also be subject to a great deal of hacking attempts from cybercriminals, endangering countless individuals and businesses in the process. More repressive nations could use a key escrow to their own nefarious spying purposes, making life for political dissidents rather challenging.

A key escrow is eventually only really effective for law enforcement in general as a global structure. Should just a handful of nations implement it, many others will follow. It's best we keep this genie in the bottle. As of 2019, only Tunisia seems to have a nationwide key escrow system in place.

The Wassenaar Arrangement

Since cryptography can be used for both benign and nefarious purposes, most governments in the early 1990s began to feel nervous about the impact the rising popularity of computing had on it. In 1995 in Wassenaar, the Netherlands, it was agreed among participating nations that a *personal use exemption* was needed for international travelers carrying encrypted devices. This exemption allows a traveler to enter a Wassenaar-compliant country with an encrypted device or two without much hassle. However, this practice requires that you do not create, share, sell, or distribute the cryptographic technology while you are there.

As of 2019, 42 countries are participating in the arrangement. So although many countries of the world have happily signed the Wassenaar Agreement, the previously mentioned rogue states did not, and neither did the countries we're about to explore in detail later in this chapter.

EU Dual-Use Controls

Basically *dual-use items* are goods, software, and technology that can be used for both civilian and military applications. The European Union has controls in place for dual-use items. Naturally, technology related to digital cryptography is considered a dual-use item. EU dual-use controls for encryption tools are influenced by the principles outlined in the Wassenaar Arrangement. General dual-use items may be traded freely within the EU, apart from some particularly sensitive items, which include nuclear materials and hazardous biological agents.

There has been a tug of war starting from 2016 between those EU states who wish to add various new categories of cyber-surveillance items to the list and those who do not. These cyber-surveillance tools would include items that "intercept mobile phones, remotely hack into computers, circumvent passwords, or identify internet users." Adding these items to the list of EU dual-use controls would probably increase the privacy level of the average European citizen to some degree as it would make access to these technologies harder for some intrusive non EU nations. However, some EU members, including Germany and France, seem to vehemently oppose this proposed action. As of 2020, the debate is still ongoing.

The Import of Cryptography

Some countries go even further than implementing strict key disclosure laws when it comes to controlling cryptography. A government has its reasons for banning the import of encryption tools made abroad. Microsoft's BitLocker software and many other such technologies aren't welcome in some jurisdictions, not without a license at least.

For one, cryptographic technology may include backdoors through which the government itself may become subject to closer scrutiny by outside actors. A populace using encrypted communication is harder to eavesdrop on even by its own intelligence agencies. Also, imported encryption tools may offer foreign powers the chance to influence a country's commerce and economy to an uncomfortable degree. Due to the aforementioned reasons, some countries prefer to have their own internal software for any cryptographic purposes.

Be aware that the countries we'll be looking into may not take too well to a tourist bringing an encrypted device at their border. If you plan to travel to these nations, bring fully unencrypted devices only to save you from questioning, detainment, and potentially fines. Devices transported across international borders may be subject to scrutiny by the government agencies at your destination. Customs officials might seize your device, duplicating its contents before handing it back to you. The device may or may not be in tip-top shape after such a procedure.

The so-called rogue states of Iran, North Korea, Sudan, and Venezuela are the most strict about having foreign cryptographic materials on their soil. Even certain operating systems might not be welcome in some of these nations. Entering these countries as a tourist with a device that has a, say, specific version of the Windows operating system with BitLocker installed might itself prove to be an issue – even if you don't possess any data encrypted with it.

Now, the following paragraphs provide a look at some of the nations with strict controls on the import of cryptographic technology. Some of this data comes from the *Electronic Privacy Information Center (EPIC)*, an independent nonprofit research center in Washington, D.C., one of the foremost authorities on the subject.

Algeria requires "all terminal equipment and radio-electric installation which is intended to be connected to a public communications network, made for the domestic market, offered for sale or distributed for free" to be approved prior to import. This almost definitely includes cryptography-related technology. The approval must be obtained from the *Regulatory Authority of Post and Electronic Communications under the Ministry of Post, Telecommunications, Technologies and Digitalization.*

In Belarus a license from the *Ministry of Foreign Affairs* or the *State Center for Information Security of the Security Council* is required to import or export cryptographic technology. Cryptography used by businesses may be subject to additional scrutiny or limitations.

China needs you to apply for a permit from the *Beijing Office of State Encryption Administrative Bureau* for any of your cryptographic needs. As of January 1st 2020, the State Council Order no 273 requires that the import and export of encryption products needs a license by the *National Commission on Encryption Code Regulations/State Cryptography Administration.* Also, be aware that electronics purchased from China may or may not contain software which spies on its users.

Egypt's *Telecommunication Regulations* prohibit "the import, manufacture or assembly of any telecommunication equipment without a license from the *National Telecom Regulatory Authority* according to the standards and specifications approved by it." This most likely applies to encryption technology as well.

The import of encryption is highly controlled in Ethiopia. The *Proclamation on Telecom Fraud Offenses* criminalizes the manufacture, assembly or import of any telecommunications equipment without a permit." This in all likelihood includes any type of encryption software. The punishment is between ten and fifteen years of "rigorous imprisonment" and a fine of between 100,000 ETB and 150,000 ETB (or between 3500 USD and 5200 USD, respectively)

Israel, while not a Wassenaar member per se, has a domestic law that adopts all Wassenaar controls automatically, including the personal use exemption for encrypted data. However, you are required to present your passwords if requested by the border security or you may face some displeasing consequences. This is to prove you are in possession of personal data only.

There has been conflicting information concerning Saudi Arabia's stance on cryptography over the years. When traveling to the country, it's best to avoid bringing encryption-related materials of any kind – and not use any when on their soil.

In Iran, a license issued by *Iran's Supreme Council for Cultural Revolution* is required. You should be aware that even if you received said license, exporting cryptographic technology from the United States to Iran violates US laws, as Iran is classified as a "state of concern."

For Kazakhstan, importing or exporting cryptographic products requires a license from the *Licensing Commission of the Committee of National Security*. Although the country hasn't signed the Wassenaar Agreement, Kazakhstan offers a personal use exemption in the spirit of said agreement; you shouldn't have an issue with an encrypted device on you over there as a tourist.

In Morocco, the import, export, or use of cryptographic technology without prior declaration is a criminal offense. Any such declarations should be addressed to the *Directorate General for Information Systems Security of Morocco*. Failing to do so is punishable by up to one year's imprisonment and a fine of up to 100,000 MAD which is around 10,400 USD.

Myanmar (formerly Burma) has a de jure penalty of five to ten years of imprisonment for acts concerning unlawful import or export of technology. And what is appropriate technology can be governed by the *Myanmar Computer Science Development Council*. There has not been a single sentencing that involved digital cryptography in Myanmar as of 2019. However, don't push your luck; it's best to not utilize encrypted data within their borders. What is known is that domestic cryptography within Myanmar requires a license.

Pakistan regulates the sale and use of cryptographic hardware and software. Such activities require an approval from *Pakistan Telecommunications Authority (PTA)*.

In Russia, a license is required for "distributing and maintaining encryption facilities, providing encryption services, and developing and manufacturing encryption facilities protected by means of encryption." These licenses are provided by the *Federal Security Service (FSB)* and possibly from the *Ministry of Economic Development and Trade* as well. Also, Russian law requires that "organizers of information distribution" add "additional coding" (i.e., backdoors) to transmitted electronic messages for the FSB to be able to decrypt them at will.

Senegal's *Law on Cryptography* simply states that "the supply or importation of a means of cryptology which does not solely perform functions of authentication and integrity control requires approval from the *National Cryptology Commission*." One should consult said agency before importing any type of encryption technology to Senegal, just to be on the safe side.

In Tunisia, a government agency called *Centre d'Etudes et de Recherches des Télécoms (CERT)* needs to examine the workings of any imported cryptographic technology. Using encryption in the country apparently requires one to hand over their passwords to the government. This seems to be an implementation of the key escrow system as discussed previously in this chapter. Domestic use of encryption is supervised by the Tunisian Ministry of Defense, while requests for a license should be sent to the *National Agency for Electronic Certification (ANCE)*.

Both the export and import of cryptographic technology in Ukraine requires a license issued by the *Department of Special Telecommunication Systems and Protection of Information of the Security Service of Ukraine (SBU)*. The country has, however, signed the Wassenaar Agreement. This means a personal use exemption is in effect.

Corporate Data Security Laws

Businesses in the United States have their digital security laws regulated by the *Federal Trade Commission (FTC)*, an independent law enforcement agency. Your business or organization is required to have specific safeguards in place to protect the privacy and personal information of your customers. If such safeguards are neglected, the FTC is obligated to seek civil monetary penalties. No business, big or small, is exempt from FTC's authority on these matters. Corporate giants Google, Facebook, and Microsoft have all been reprimanded by the agency in recent years. In short, organizations of all sizes should have a dedicated security officer to oversee all matters relating to data security – and use strong encryption for their users' data. Leave no customer dataset unencrypted.

The FTC Safeguards Rule

While the FTC isn't exactly easy on any type of business, its requirements for privacy are even stricter for financial institutions. A perhaps surprising amount of businesses fall under this classification, including not only banks or check-cashing companies but also mortgage brokers, real estate appraisers, professional tax preparers, and even courier services. These stricter privacy policies for financial institutions are collectively known as the *FTC Safeguards Rule*. Again, the size of the business is irrelevant; the agency monitors all.

The FTC Safeguards Rule took effect in 2003 and continues to be the gold standard for customer privacy with frequent amendments. Its main requirements include the following:

- The business should have one or more employees to coordinate its information security program.

- Risks to customer information in each relevant area of the company's operation should be identified.

- The effectiveness of the current safeguards for controlling these risks should be evaluated on a regular basis.

- Continued evaluation of the program in light of relevant circumstances, including changes in the firm's business or operations or the results of security testing and monitoring.

Some hands-on solutions recommended by the FTC include the following:

- **The usage of strong passwords at all times** (i.e., requiring passwords with at least six characters, consisting of upper- and lowercase letters, numbers, and symbols)

- **Using password-activated screensavers which lock up a device after a period of inactivity.**

- **Making sure employees store mobile devices in a secure place when not in use.** Also, making sure the data on these devices is encrypted whenever possible.

- **Using discretion when allowing an employee to access customer data from outside of the workplace (i.e., telecommuting).** This includes having employees install the latest anti-malware software on their remote workstations.

- **Disabling access to any user data from former employees immediately after termination.**

- **Protecting the servers containing user data from physical hazards such as fire or flooding.**

Organizations are given a fairly large degree of flexibility by the FTC on how they follow the Safeguards Rule. Cryptographic and other technological solutions aside, businesses are also recommended to perform background checks on all of their potential employees and having them sign confidentiality agreements. All passwords within an organization's systems within the reach of a terminated employee should be changed when said employee is terminated. Also, information inside an organization should be kept compartmentalized at all times and transferred between groups on a need-to-know basis.

For any medium or large business, security testers (i.e., paid hackers) should be hired to evaluate your systems' defensive capabilities against cyberattacks. Vulnerability scans can be performed by a small team; these usually consist of the use of various types of vulnerability scanner software. The next stage in security testing consists of penetration tests. This is basically a controlled hacking situation, where the tester does his or her very best to enter a system, naturally without causing any actual damage to the business. The results of these processes may end up saving your organization quite a bit of money in the long term and should be thus prioritized high.

More on Privacy Laws in the United States

Like you probably know by now, **digital privacy laws** refer to the privacy of communication and individualized data in a digital, often online context. **Medical privacy laws** deal with the use of patient records and an individual's genetic material. **Financial privacy laws** address how companies process financial consumer data.

Table 7-1 lists some of the most relevant pieces of US federal legislation for each category of data. All of these acts have a great deal to do with you and your organization's privacy; the bigger your business grows, the more you should know about all of them.

Table 7-1. *Most relevant US federal legislation for privacy*

Digital Privacy	Medical Privacy	Financial Privacy
Cyber Intelligence Sharing and Protection Act of 2015 (CISPA)	Health Information Technology for Economic and Clinical Health Act (HITECH)	Fair Credit Reporting Act
Electronic Communications Privacy Act	Genetic Information Nondiscrimination Act (GINA)	Electronic Funds Transfer Act
Economic Espionage Act	Health Insurance Portability and Accountability Act (HIPAA)	Fair Debt Collection Practices Act
Computer Fraud and Abuse Act	The Privacy Act of 1974	Bank Secrecy Act

A Few Words on CISPA

The *Cyber Intelligence Sharing and Protection Act* (which finally passed in 2015 after some years in limbo) is a rather controversial piece of legislation. Its opponents criticize the act for allowing eavesdropped, private communications to be handed over to the government without warrants. Vocal critics of CISPA include former Representative Ron Paul, the Electronic Freedom Foundation (EFF), and the over 840,000 people who signed an online petition at *Avaaz.org*.

However, CISPA is not without support among some major companies; these include *Microsoft*, *IBM*, and *AT&T*. Supporters for the act have stated it provides streamlined means for delivering potentially critical information to the right officials. In fact, a total of over 800 companies have voiced their support for CISPA.

State-Level Privacy Legislation

Privacy laws vary greatly from state to state within the United States. Many states have recently passed new legislation in numerous varieties of privacy laws. State laws typically complement federal laws, which are applied nationwide.

Interestingly, California is extremely serious about digital privacy with its 12 major pieces of related legislation, perhaps due to being the most populous state in the United States – and housing some major corporations. The *California Consumer Privacy Act of 2018* caused quite a bit of stress among the bigger businesses in order to satisfy the growing privacy needs of the people, who now have an opportunity to opt out of certain data collection practices.

Now, should you travel or do business in the United States, you might benefit from an overview of the types of privacy-related legislation categories currently in effect. Table 7-2 shows the major emphases in US statewide legislation at a glance. Note: The S character signifies a particularly strong set of laws in a specific field, with seven or more pieces of state legislation in effect as of 2020.

Table 7-2. *An overview of US privacy-related laws*

State	State Law(s) in Effect	State	State Law(s) in Effect
Alabama	Medical, data privacy, financial	**Montana**	Data privacy, digital
Alaska	Medical, data security, financial	**Nebraska**	Medical, digital
Arizona	Medical (S), digital	**Nevada**	Medical, digital
Arkansas	Medical, digital	**New Hampshire**	Medical (S), digital
California	Medical, digital (S), financial	**New Mexico**	Medical (S), digital
Colorado	Medical, digital, financial	**New York**	Medical
Connecticut	Digital	**N. Carolina**	Medical, data privacy
Delaware	Medical, digital	**N. Dakota**	Medical, data privacy
Florida	Medical, digital	**Ohio**	Data privacy
Georgia	Medical	**Oklahoma**	Medical, digital
Hawaii	Medical	**Oregon**	Medical, digital

(*continued*)

Table 7-2. (*continued*)

State	State Law(s) in Effect	State	State Law(s) in Effect
Idaho	Medical	Pennsylvania	Medical, digital
Illinois	Medical (S), digital	Rhode Island	Medical (S), digital
Indiana	Digital	S. Carolina	Medical
Iowa	Medical (S)	S. Dakota	Medical
Kansas	Medical	Tennessee	Medical, digital
Kentucky	Medical	Texas	Medical
Louisiana	Medical, digital	Utah	Medical, digital
Maine	Medical, digital	Vermont	Medical, digital, financial
Maryland	Medical (S), digital	Virginia	Medical, digital
Massachusetts	Medical, digital	Washington	Medical, digital
Michigan	Medical (S), digital	West Virginia	Medical, digital
Minnesota	Medical, digital	Wisconsin	Digital privacy
Mississippi	Medical	Wyoming	Medical
Missouri	Medical, digital		

A Primer on US Legal Terms

If you are a non-US citizen, you may need to brush up on some legal terminology in use in the region. This section is just what you need in that case.

A subpoena is also called *a witness summons*, and it simply refers to a written order provided by a court of law which compels an individual to either provide (a) a witness testimony or (b) some other type of evidence, under a penalty. The former is known in Latin as *subpoena ad testificandum*, while the latter is called *subpoena duces tecum*.

A grand jury is a group between 16 and 23 citizens who listen to evidence of criminal allegations, presented by the prosecutors, and determine whether probable cause exists to believe an individual has committed an offense. As of 2019, grand juries are only used in the United States and the Republic of Liberia.

The *United States courts of appeals*, also referred to as *circuit courts*, decide appeals from *district courts*, which in turn are the general trial courts. There are 13 courts of appeals in the United States, each usually presiding over a specific geographic area spanning several states. For example, the US Court of Appeals for the Tenth Circuit covers appeals in Colorado, Kansas, New Mexico, Oklahoma, Utah, and Wyoming. However, the 13th court of appeals, the *Federal Circuit*, has nationwide jurisdiction over specific appeals defined by special subject matter.

Contempt of court refers to the offensive act of being disrespectful toward a court of law and its members. There are two ways a person can be found in contempt of court: he or she can either display disruptive behavior toward the legal authorities in the courtroom, or merely fail to obey a court order.

De jure is a term in Latin which refers to practices signed into law that are not necessarily enforced in any way. *De facto* stands for practices that are not a part of any legislation, but take frequently place regardless.

An Executive Order is an instruction (i.e., a directive) of the President of the United States that operates on the Federal level and carries the force of law. Although the US Constitution lacks a provision that addresses the use of executive orders per se, the term is mentioned as the instruction to "take Care that the Laws be faithfully executed" in Article II. The US Supreme Court has decided that all executive orders from the president must be supported by the Constitution. Executive orders can be blocked by the Congress or the Federal courts, but they rarely are. The *Office of the Federal Register* is responsible for issuing executive orders in their sequential numbers. The current record holder for most executive orders issued remains with President *Franklin D. Roosevelt* who, during his exceptional three terms in office, made 3522 orders.

Reasonable suspicion is one of two major legal standards in the United States which govern the actions of certain government officials, such as border security and the police. It refers to as what a reasonable person (i.e., the average person) would consider suspicious. Reasonable suspicion was solidified in US law with the landmark case of *Terry v. Ohio* in 1968 by the Supreme Court. The other main legal standard is **probable cause**, which deals with arrests and warrants; it's mentioned in the Fourth Amendment to the US Constitution. Out of these two standards, *reasonable suspicion* allows for searches, but not handcuffing, arrests, or other more drastic measures.

In Closing

After finishing this chapter, you should be informed on the following:

- Key disclosure laws in the United States and abroad

- How the importation of cryptographic technology is viewed by foreign jurisdictions

- What the *FTC Safeguards Rule* is and when it's applicable

- What the most relevant US federal privacy laws are as well as an overview of US state-level privacy laws

The next chapter will take us into the world of quantum mechanics. We'll explore topics such as qubits and superposition. Excited? You should be!

CHAPTER 8

Quantum Computing: The Next Big Paradigm

As well established and world changing as the digital revolution has been, its days are numbered. The never-ending march of scientific progress will deliver us a new paradigm in the very near future: quantum computing. Its applications, while at first purely theoretical, will eventually cover many aspects of our lives: communications, medicine, security, and even world politics. In this chapter we'll take a glance at some of the ramifications of quantum computing before moving into specifics with the chapters to follow.

Bits vs. Qubits

For the past century all computing devices have basically used the same approach of binary code. Although there have been many varieties of computing architectures, they have all shared this fundamental method of operation. However, within the next ten to fifteen years, this is going to change radically.

© Robert Ciesla 2020
R. Ciesla, *Encryption for Organizations and Individuals*,
https://doi.org/10.1007/978-1-4842-6056-2_8

Now, in quantum computing the smallest unit of measurement is called a *quantum bit* or a *qubit*. Classical computing, that is, binary code, uses either zeros and ones, while qubit units utilize a phenomenon called *superposition* to occupy both zero and one at the same time. Qubits are therefore two-state units by nature, operating in a continuum of changing values. This has enormous implications for calculations of any kind. The century of silicone chips and traditional binary computing is coming to an end just as the era of vacuum tube computers did before that.

Into the Bloch Sphere

Quantum superposition found in qubits is often demonstrated using a Bloch sphere (see Figure 8-1). You don't need to grasp this figure just yet; for now, a quick glance is enough. We'll delve much deeper into what the implications of quantum physics actually are in the next chapter. For now, just know this: quantum mechanics is a fundamental theory of physics within the realm of sub-atomic particles representing a wondrous paradoxical world of curiosities.

However, if you're interested in some of the inner workings of qubits, read on. If not, feel free to skip to the section titled "Six Ways Qubits Will Change Our World."

Classical/Digital Bit

Represents either 1 or 0

Quantum Bit (Qubit)

Represents both 1 and 0
via *superposition*

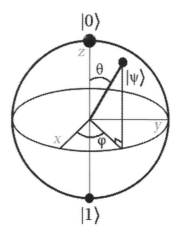

Figure 8-1. *A geometrical representation of a qubit known as the "Bloch sphere" in which two states (0 and 1) are represented by vectors $|0\rangle$ and $|1\rangle$. The diagram was devised by physicist* **Felix Bloch** *(1905–1983)*

Physically qubits can take the form of single electrons, pulled right out of an atom. When left to their own devices, qubits contain probabilities for delivering the value of one (1) or zero (0). Upon observation using a powerful electron microscope, the qubit will stick to representing one of those values; in quantum physics, the act of observation alone defines the outcome.

Now, a *vector* is a quantity with direction and size. If you were to travel north from your current location with the speed of, say, 12 km per hour for an hour, that dataset would constitute a vector. Similarly, vectors are key ingredients in specifying quantum superposition. Qubits are represented using *Bloch vectors*. These are unit vectors (i.e., vectors with the upper length of 1) used to indicate points within the Bloch sphere. The one/zero state of the qubit is represented by the point where the vector collides with the surface of the sphere. The Bloch sphere also represents a qubit's phase information using rotation around the Z axis.

In the Bloch sphere from Figure 8-1, the symbol θ (theta) represents a point's co-latitude with respect to the z axis, while the φ (phi) represents longitude along the x axis, specifying a point in the sphere. States zero and one are displayed as vectors $|0\rangle$ and $|1\rangle$ on the top and bottom areas of the sphere, respectively. Make note of $|\psi\rangle$ (psi): it's there to represent the superposition of these vectors/states.

Bra-ket notation refers to the practice of using specific symbols like the angle brackets and the vertical bar to denote vectors such as quantum states. You may have spotted the use of this system in some of the previous paragraphs in this chapter. Invented by theoretical physicist *Paul Dirac* in 1939, bra-ket notation is sometimes also referred to as *Dirac notation*.

A Bloch sphere demonstrates that a qubit must be represented using two *complex numbers* which, in turn, consist of *real numbers* and *imaginary numbers*. Bloch vectors are always complex numbers.

Here's a refresher on the different types of numbers we've touched on so far:

- **Real numbers** are basically any number one can come up with on the spot (e.g., *30, 5.2, -4.4*). Squared real numbers, even when negative, give a positive result (e.g., *5 x 5 = 25, -4 x -4 = 16*). A unit of a real number is simply 1.

- **Imaginary numbers** give a negative result when squared (and yes, they are not actually that imaginary). A unit of this type of number is the square root of -1 as in $\sqrt{(-1)}$. For example, *4i* is an imaginary number (*-4 x -4* where *i x i =-1* results in *-16*).

- **Complex numbers** are combinations of real and imaginary numbers. They follow the form $a + bi$, where a is a real number and b is an imaginary number. Again, the "i" represents the solution of the equation $x^2 = -1$. Examples of complex numbers include $27 + 3i$, $-4.1 + 1.9i$, and $3.2 + 1.3i$.

A series of interconnected qubits can express numerous different values at the same time using superposition. This is why quantum devices are untold times more powerful than classical digital units at virtually any type of calculations. Increasing the number of qubits in a quantum-based device has an exponential effect on its computing power. That quickly adds to a lot of computational capacity. Quantum computers can also store data more densely than their silicone-based brethren. This experimental technique is known as *superdense coding*.

Six Ways Qubits Will Change Our World

We'll next explore the main realms in which our world might change forever as quantum computing is gradually introduced in the near future. The following scenarios are mostly based on some educated guesses by the author.

Cryptography

One field perhaps most obviously revolutionized by the looming quantum revolution will be cryptography. The world of sub-atomic particles offers both powerful new levels of security and detrimental effects on the integrity of current-generation encryption schemes, many of which will be compromised. However, panic need not set in just yet. At least for the first few generations, quantum-based computers are unlikely to do terminal damage to encryption algorithms not based on prime numbers, such as the puissant Advanced Encryption Standard (AES). However, some of their weaker brethren (i.e., the 128-bit varieties) are likely to become considerably more susceptible to brute-force attacks; quantum computers can process massive amounts of data per cycle compared to their silicone-based equivalents.

As will be discussed in detail later in the book, the field of quantum cryptography won't be only used to hack older algorithms; it will also bring about new and potentially unbreakable methods of encryption and data transmission. While not an actual encryption method, *quantum key distribution (QKD)* is a closely related concept which we'll cover in detail in the chapters to come. QKD is meant to only provide secure passwords for use in tandem with a traditional encryption scheme, such as the AES, constituting a hybrid approach. Key distribution aside, there are a number of bona fide quantum encryption algorithms in development, one of the better known being the *Kak's three-stage protocol* devised by accomplished computer scientist *Subhash Kak*.

Medicine

There is little doubt quantum computing will usher in a new era in medicine. Medical simulations can be performed at speeds unheard of until then. Unfazed due to the massive financial incentives involved, big pharma will be happy to invest in quantum computing. New medications will be introduced at a much faster rate due to greatly reduced time needed on clinical trials. Medical schools will delight at the opportunities provided by new resources and teaching methods. This works also in reducing the costs of medical training from the students' point of view in some instances.

At some point virtual beings will be created; these will be equal to their real-life counterparts for most, if not all, medical purposes. Operating on a sub-atomic level, quantum-based technology will be introduced as a cure for some illnesses considered terminal as of today. A massively accelerated sequencing of human DNA is another opportunity offered by quantum computing. Biological immortality may or may not become attainable for the wealthiest, at least. As with all technology, there will be a dark side to quantum computing. Qubit-based technology might be used for engineering new biological threats, such as resistant-treatment diseases, for use by rogue actors.

In quantum science the act of observing sub-atomic events actually changes their outcome. *Quantum immortality* is a thought experiment in this realm. Basically it purports to a theoretical scenario in which a lethal device is either used or not used on a human being based on the outcome of a single quantum-level event. Generally, the term "quantum immortality" is not to be used when discussing the potential of, say, quantum-based medicine in achieving actual immortality as we usually know it.

Crime and Finance

As current-era encryption algorithms become more fragile in the near future, cybercriminals will look to quantum-based approaches out of necessity. A minor crisis of cybercrime will take place as soon as the first wave of quantum computers become mainstream. For one, traditional types of ransomware simply won't cut it as private security firms and/ or law enforcement will eventually be armed with a new generation of cryptographic tools, that is, quantum-based code breakers. Before any shady actors develop functional quantum cryptanalyses (i.e., anti-quantum solutions), there will be a lull in espionage and data theft as well. The countermeasures against legitimate quantum encryption probably arrive with a delay of a few years at least.

Hacking and code breaking aside, the most imminent problems potentially accelerated by quantum computing reside in the global financial sector. Stock markets and their associated shareholders might find themselves in an unpleasant warm substance as quantum-powered market manipulation and a new breed of white-collar crime become a reality.

Blockchains vs. Qubits

A *blockchain* is a collection of data records/blocks that are linked using cryptographic means. By nature of their design, blockchains are in most cases immune to tampering by third-party actors prior, during, and after transmission. Blockchains are utilized in cryptocurrencies (such as *Bitcoin*) and in distributed ledger technology by several global financial institutions.

Now, cryptocurrencies have been hard to regulate at times and they've thus proposed a threat to suppliers of traditional financial instruments. The age of quantum computers may actually end this tug of war in favor of well-established banking institutions. For one, it has been proposed the technology will break the once-venerable Rivest–Shamir–Adleman (RSA) algorithm and others, backbones of many blockchains including Bitcoin, rendering these currencies unusable. Quantum computing offers potentially several new attack vectors against users of cryptocurrencies, so hold on to your virtual wallets and keep an eye on this particular quantum-based threat.

Blockchain technology was released to public by an individual (or group) known as *Satoshi Nakamoto* in 2008. This is most likely a pseudonym created for reasons yet unknown.

Entertainment

A boom in quantum-based entertainment is to be expected. Today's relatively sophisticated 3D video games will look crude compared to those powered with processors dishing out several orders of magnitude more of processing power. This may cause issues with addiction-prone individuals as a new lifelike wave of immersive entertainment will no doubt hook many. New virtual and augmented reality applications in particular can completely take over a vulnerable gamer's life. If unchecked, such a scenario might take a toll on the productivity, tax base, and overall stability of afflicted societies. After all, as of 2020 countries like Japan and South Korea continue to have a major problem with swathes of young people dropping out and opting to play current-generation video games en masse while contributing to society in a diminished manner. In a 2019 survey, it was estimated that Japan has over 1 million unemployed recluses, or *hikikomori* (Kyodo News, 2019). Also, according to Japan's government-run National Institute of Population and Social Security Research, one-person households will reach a total 39% by 2040 (Osumi, 2018). With no family to take care of, electronic entertainment is likely to play a big part in a Japanese single person's daily activities.

Manufacturing

There is no doubt quantum computing will revolutionize manufacturing. The numerous applications of this technology include new power sources, elaborate risk modeling, advanced robotics, and rapid calculations/ simulations of extremely high precision. All this may also result in less strain on the environment as power consumption and waste management in the manufacturing sector is eventually optimized, proving ecologically superior to current approaches. We can expect a leap forward in industrial design and product safety, too. As these are still the early years of quantum-based computing, most businesses will be wary of jumping into the fray. However, as more and more hungry startups and established brands take on this technology, the temptation to go quantum will become irresistible for even the most stubborn of companies; in the very near future, the risks will become negligible, outweighed by benefits in every metric.

In recent years, industry giants *IBM*, *Microsoft*, *Intel*, and *Google* have begun investing in quantum computing in earnest. Many other companies not open about their research are likely to have their quantum-based projects listed as "skunkworks" with semi-clandestine special teams working for the sake of innovation, free from the ferrous grip of management.

World Politics

Sooner or later some serious political implications will arise when considering all of the preceding effects of the quantum revolution. Basically, quantum computing is the nuclear arms race of the twenty-first century. The regime which develops the first fully functional quantum system has the potential means to annihilate even the most secure of encryption, such as the AES-256, in a matter of months instead of billions of years as per classical computing devices. Espionage and related paranoia will reach untold levels when this scenario unfolds. Of course, belligerent nations in charge of a theoretical quantum supercomputer are unlikely to advertise its existence until one day all of our banking systems and state secrets are in jeopardy. In the wrong hands the quantum revolution could even accelerate a global military conflict.

In Closing

After finishing this chapter, you will have learned the following:

- How quantum computing differs from classical computing and what *qubits* refer to

- What vectors, imaginary numbers, and the Bloch sphere are and how they relate to quantum computing

- Which six far-reaching effects quantum computing has on the world

In the next chapter we'll take a more comprehensive look at the numerous implications of quantum mechanics, exploring the many ways it changed our understanding of the world.

References

Kyodo News. 2019. Japan Times. Retrieved from: www.japantimes.co.jp/news/2019/03/29/national/613000-japan-aged-40-64-recluses-says-first-government-survey-hikikomori/

Osumi, Magdalena. 2018. Many of Japan's growing number of singles claim they are comfortable facing death alone. Japan Times. Retrieved from: www.japantimes.co.jp/news/2018/06/14/national/social-issues/many-japans-growing-number-singles-claim-comfortable-facing-death-alone/

CHAPTER 9

The Rollicking World of Quantum Mechanics

Deepening one's knowledge on quantum mechanics and related physics paves the way for a greater understanding of the definite future of computing and cryptography. Quantum mechanics is a branch of physics focusing on the smallest scales known to us: the atomic and the sub-atomic realms. It has numerous implications for our world, as discussed in the previous chapter, and it comes with some controversy as well. We'll now go more or less clavicle deep into this sub-atomic level and explore its numerous paradigm-shifting phenomena.

A Few Words on Classical Mechanics

There are roughly two spheres of physics: classical and modern. The former consists of methods dealing mostly with the motion of visible objects (such as arrows, apples, and galaxies), while the latter deals with phenomena and attributes on the scale of a much smaller, sub-atomic world. Of course, modern physics don't exist in a vacuum; they do build on the foundation of classical mechanics.

© Robert Ciesla 2020
R. Ciesla, *Encryption for Organizations and Individuals*,
https://doi.org/10.1007/978-1-4842-6056-2_9

One of the most monumental works of classical physics, *Philosophiae Naturalis Principia Mathematica*, was authored by **Sir Isaac Newton** all the way back in 1687. With this trilogy of books, Sir Newton codified some of the core laws of physics which not surprisingly became known as *Newton's laws of motion*. These are as follows:

- **Newton's first law (the law of inertia).** An object either remains at rest or continues to move at a constant speed unless acted upon by an external force.

- **Newton's second law.** An object, with the constant mass of m, is influenced by force F, which gives it the acceleration rate a. The greater the force, the greater the acceleration. This is formulated as $F = ma$.

- **Newton's third law (the action–reaction law).** Whenever a body exerts a force on a second body, the second body exerts a force equal in magnitude, but in the opposite direction on the first body. In other words, for every action there is an equal and opposite reaction.

Another fundamental Newton's law exists: *the law of gravitation*. This tenet laid the foundations for *superposition*, which was described in Chapter 8. Some refer to this law as *Newton's fourth law*. However, it's best to only refer to the first three as Newton's laws; these axioms allowed us to operate with experimental data while also playing an epistemological role in classical physics. Newton's law of gravitation is a different beast as it provided, for the first time, the means of calculating a fundamental force (Newburgh, Ronald. 2001. *Phys. Educ.* 36, 202).

Epistemology is the study of the nature of knowledge. It deals with questions like "what are the limits of human knowledge?" and "what is the truth?".

Introducing Modern Physics

Modern physics is sometimes referred to as *post-Newtonian physics*. This branch of mechanics has basically two cornerstones: quantum mechanics and **Albert Einstein's** theory of relativity. This theory in turn consists of two components: *special relativity* and *general relativity*. The former describes the relationship between space and time. The latter is a theory of gravitation, building on Isaac Newton's law of universal gravitation. What follows are the main discoveries of the aforementioned two theories in a thoroughly condensed form.

Einstein's theory of *special relativity* in a considerably small nutshell:

- Published in 1905, this is the generally accepted and confirmed theory about the relationship between space and time.

- Special relativity basically consists of two axioms:

    1. The laws of physics are identical in all resting frames of reference (i.e., when objects are not acted upon by external forces).

    2. The speed of light in a vacuum is the same for all observers, regardless of the movement of the light source or that of the observer.

- The famous equation $E = mc^2$ (i.e., the *mass–energy equivalence formula*) is often attributed to Einstein's theory of special relativity. It reads "energy equals mass multiplied by the speed of light (c) squared." The formula denotes a connection between energy (E) and mass (m); anything with mass has an equivalent amount of energy and vice versa.

$E = mc^2$ is actually short for $E^2=(mc^2)^2+(pc)^2$. For the sake of brevity, the equation is usually displayed in its simplified and thus more media-friendly form. Oh, and the p in the longer form stands for momentum.

Einstein's *theory of general relativity* in another very tiny shell:
Next up is a condensed version of the other seminal Einstein's theory.

- Published in 1915, this is Einstein's comprehensive theory on gravity.

- General relativity expands on the theory of special relativity by including areas/masses that are accelerating in relation to each other. The interaction between mass and space-time is what constitutes our understanding of gravitation.

- The theory consists of specific *field equations*, which are used to represent the dynamics of changes in time and space distribution. These are usually referred to as *Einstein field equations (EFEs)*.

- General relativity shows that light follows a so-called "curvature in space-time" as it passes bigger celestial objects, such as neutron stars and black holes. The latter are areas of exceptionally strong gravitational forces from which not even light can escape. Black holes are thought to form when very large stars collapse.

Classical physics can explain many workings of the universe. However, it has some blind spots so it's not without issues. We won't address these in detail as that is outside of the scope of this book. It's sufficient to say classical mechanics work great on a large enough scale (i.e., the macro-scale), but less so in the smaller realms of existence. When it comes to the micro-side of things, that's where quantum mechanics comes to shine and that's where we're headed next.

Atoms and Sub-atomic Particles

Let's now take a somewhat closer look at sub-atomic particles and how they've known to behave in the quantum realm. This way we'll be expanding our knowledge on qubits (as discussed in the previous chapter), for one.

Now, atoms were once thought to be the smallest unit of matter. At roughly tenth-millionth of a millimeter, they most certainly are quite small. In fact, classical physics cannot accurately predict an atom's behavior. As science and engineering progressed over time, we began to reach scales of matter much smaller than the atomic one. The smallest type of particles that we're currently able to study is known as *elementary particles*. Atoms consist of electrons, protons, and neutrons. All atoms are formed from the elementary particles.

Their diminutive size notwithstanding, these particles have some rather peculiar properties. One of them, called *spin* (usually denoted with *S*), refers to the angular momentum intrinsic to elementary particles. Unlike, say, a bowling ball, a sub-atomic particle never actually stops spinning. You can make it change direction, but you'll have a hard time bringing it to a halt. Spin in the sub-atomic world is an immutable quality, like mass or charge. Think of elementary particles as mathematical points in time space. Table 9-1 shows a partial table of known sub-atomic particles.

Table 9-1. *A partial table of known sub-atomic particles, mass and charge not included*

The Fermions				The Bosons	
	First generation	**Second generation**	**Third generation**		
Quarks	Up	Charm	Top	Gluon	Higgs (spin 0)
	Down	Strange	Bottom	Photon	
Leptons	Electron	Muon	Tau	Z boson	
	Electron neutrino	Muon neutrino	Tau neutrino	W boson	

Now, the first major group of elementary particles is known as the *fermions*. They have been given rather exotic names, such as "charm," "strange," and "bottom." These are sometimes known as *flavors*. The fermions are divided into *quarks* and *leptons*; all fermions have a spin value of ½. The second major group of elementary particles, the bosons, carry a spin value of 1, save for the rather recently discovered Higgs boson which has a spin of 0 (zero).

The fermions are also often categorized by their generation. Each generation in general has more mass than the previous one (e.g., up quarks have less mass than top quarks).

Black Holes and Their Applications

Black holes aren't just a sci-fi trope. For one, they potentially offer incredible sources of energy ripe for harvesting as soon as the technology is there. If our scientists and engineers one day manage to leverage the power of a black hole, we would basically enter a new golden age of technology.

The average black hole is relatively small at roughly 30 kilometers in diameter. *Supermassive black holes*, also known as *quasars*, are a different beast at around 125 billion kilometers in diameter. They emit enormous amounts of energy, probably contributing to the rate of star formation within a galaxy (Hopkins, Hernquist, L., Cox, T. J. et al. 2006).

Yet another class of black holes are the *primordial black holes*. The formation of these types of archaic black holes is due to a fluctuation in the density of the universe, inducing its gravitational collapse. Coming into existence in under a second after the *Big Bang*, primordial black holes have much less mass than their younger brethren; they are theorized to be some 10^{-5} grams in mass in their smallest variety (Klesman, 2019).

Now, a so-called no-hair theorem states that after formation a black hole has only three physical properties: mass, angular momentum, and charge. Any other information present during a black hole's formation is simply destroyed. Therefore, black holes sharing the same values for these properties are thought to be indistinguishable. Whether this theorem holds true in reality is yet to be confirmed.

It wasn't until 2019 when scientists actually managed to photograph a black hole using a synchronized array of eight telescopes stationed around various parts of our planet. The resulting at-first modest seeming image of an orange blob carries a lot of significance.

Through the *Hubble Space Telescope*, we can currently observe about a hundred billion galaxies, a number which may represent a very small amount of the total. It's very likely that most galaxies have a massive black hole at their center. Let's now go through the basic regions of these glorious theoretical masses in space (see Figure 9-1).

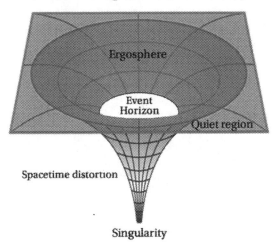

The Main Regions in a Black Hole

Figure 9-1. *The main regions in a black hole visualized*

The Quiet Region and the Ergosphere

The *quiet region* is a geometric area where bodies of mass shouldn't have much difficulty in pulling away from the center of a black hole: no need to break the limits of the speed of light here. Now, in an *ergosphere* the forces of gravity slowly start to go into overdrive. However, objects not too close to the event horizon can still escape this region. The size of an ergosphere is deemed to be proportional to a black hole's gravitational strength and angular momentum (i.e., its quantity of rotation).

An ergosphere is sometimes confused with the *accretion disk*. This is a disk formed of particles orbiting the black hole, while the ergosphere refers to the broader region surrounding it. Black hole accretion disks often consist of matter in the x-ray part of the spectrum.

The Event Horizon (No, Not the 1990s Movie)

These days somewhat a part of the general discourse, an *event horizon* refers to a boundary beyond which events cannot influence observers. The term is often used when describing the immediate area around black holes. The only way to pull yourself out of this area would to travel faster than the speed of light. This isn't possible according to current understanding. After entering the event horizon, you're well on your way into a theorized singularity.

Now, the physical radius of an event horizon surrounding a nonrotating black hole is known as the *Schwarzschild radius*. This concept also defines that *any* object with a radius smaller than its Schwarzschild radius is to be a black hole.

Singularity Speculation

Inside the black hole lurks the mighty *singularity*. This is basically an unknown region of infinite density as described by Einstein's theory of general relativity; the further inside you go, the more distortion in space-time you would experience. Laws of physics break down inside singularities (hence all the speculation about these things in science fiction). However, there are some differing voices to the very existence of this phenomenon; some scientists insist singularities as per Einstein's theories are flawed.

A new paradigm regarding black holes and their singularities is emerging in the scientific community. This is known as *loop quantum gravity*. Basically, this new theory introduces a new powerful repulsive force which is able to counteract the pull of a black hole. Loop quantum gravity isn't a replacement for general relativity, rather, it builds on its principles (Sholtis, 2019).

In 2006 *Dr. Manjir Samanta-Laughton* proposed a new theory called *The Black Hole Principle* for the workings of the universe. Her book *Punk Science* introduced the idea that black holes actually introduce energy into our universe instead of merely absorbing it. Also according to Dr. Samanta-Laughton, black holes exist pretty much everywhere, including inside living organisms. Although the jury is out, there is some evidence for parts of this theory.

Perhaps our gravitationally talented friends lurking in outer space aren't indeed as destructive as we think. It has been postulated that a black hole computer is feasible in the future. There are types of photons (i.e., light particles) constantly being emitted around black holes in an area known as an *accretion disk*. When escaping this area and experiencing radical changes to their angle of polarization and orbital angular momentum, these particles display properties which could eventually be harnessed for quantum computing (Racorean, 2018, p. 254-264).

Needless to say, this would give us an incredible amount of data storage and computing power, putting any run-of-the-mill quantum computer to shame. At that point we might have 100% secure communications on our hands, for one.

The Standard Model

It's generally thought there are four *fundamental forces* at work in the universe from the physics point of view. These are as follows:

- **The electromagnetic force.** All electrically charged particles manifest this force. It's the binding "glue" that keeps molecules together. The electromagnetic force is responsible for all chemical processes between interactions of the electrons in neighboring atoms. And how do magnets work? Through this particular force, of course.

- **The weak nuclear force.** This force governs the radioactive decay of atoms as well as serving an important role in nuclear fission. For one, the sun is powered by the processes manifested by the weak nuclear force. This force can also change a sub-atomic particle of one type into a completely different one.

- **The strong nuclear force.** All ordinary matter in the universe is thought to be held together by this force. Like its name implies, this is one formidable power. Interestingly, the strong nuclear force is most potent the closer its governed bodies (i.e., sub-atomic particles) remain.

- **Gravity.** This force, unfamiliar to none, holds planets and galaxies in their orbits. And should a chunky middle-aged man jump on a trampoline, you'd see just what gravity is capable of. While this may sound like a formidable force, and it is, under most daily scenarios, gravity is actually the weakest of the four. For example, if you want to counteract Earth's gravitational pull, just lift that apple that fell off the ground.

In the mid-1970s, the term *Standard Model* was coined to describe the unified scientific theory describing three of the aforementioned forces; it hasn't incorporated gravity as of yet. If the gravitational force was somehow integrated into the other force theories, we would get a so-called theory of everything (TOE).

There're also some murmurs about a potential fifth fundamental force. This would cover the so-called dark matter. Well over half of our known universe is estimated to be made of this mysterious energy (Baudis 2012, p.94-108). It's called dark matter because it doesn't seem to interact with the electromagnetic spectrum, including visible light, in that many ways. Being so hard to detect, dark matter is a mostly theorized element. Therefore, a fifth fundamental force is yet to gain wide approval in the global scientific community; we're stuck with four forces for the time being.

Dark matter is not the same as *dark energy*, which is still a related concept. Dark energy refers to another mostly theoretical force which has been used to explain the accelerating rate at which the universe seems to be expanding. Postulated by many scientists in the past, this phenomenon was confirmed in 1998 by two award-winning multinational research teams.

A Brief History of the Higgs Boson

Named after British physicist *Peter Higgs*, this elusive boson was finally discovered in 2012 using the *Large Hadron Collider* at the *Conseil Européen pour la Recherche Nucléaire (CERN)*. The Higgs boson was an until-then theorized elementary particle that would complete the picture on how particles have mass in the first place.

The Higgs boson is not surprisingly closely related to the *Higgs field*; this refers to a universal quantum field that separates massless particles into those with mass. In this, all-pervasive field particles are issued mass using a so-called Higgs mechanism.

A popular analogy for the Higgs field is to think of the functioning of a prism. When issued one type of white light, the glass projects multiple bands of color. More accurately put, the Higgs boson operates using a phenomenon known as *spontaneous symmetry breaking*.

Mainstream media has rather pompously dubbed the Higgs boson "The God Particle" to the dismay of some. However, this boson is quite revelatory and might pave the way for understanding the mysteries of dark matter, for one.

More Quantum Magic

As discussed in the previous chapter, there are a fair number of interesting properties to sub-atomic particles. Now, you should take a relatively deep breath before proceeding with the chapter.

The Uncertainty Principle

Presented in 1927 by German physicist **Werner Heisenberg** (1901–1976), the *uncertainty principle* basically states that the more precision is used for the measurement of one property of a particle (e.g., its mass), the less precise the calculation of an associated property becomes (e.g., its position). In other words, you can't know everything about a system even using the approaches of quantum physics. The *double-slit experiment*, discussed next, is an apt way to demonstrate the uncertainty principle in action.

Double-Slit Experiments: The Wave–Particle Duality

A phenomenon known as *wave–particle duality* is central to quantum mechanics. It states that every quantum entity can be approached either as a particle or a wave. Upon discovery this caused some confusion as it isn't quite what classical particle physics stated. As Einstein stated, we suddenly had two contradictory views on reality; when separated, neither can offer a satisfactory explanation for the workings of light, for one, but put together they certainly can.

Now, sub-atomic particles simply exhibit two different behaviors: that of a particle or that of a wave. An experiment known as the *double-slit experiment* demonstrated this. Devised in 1801 by physicist **Thomas Young** (1773–1829), this experiment at first dealt with light-related properties only. It was further refined by numerous scientists a century or so later to include electrons, atoms, and molecules. Basically, in the double-slit experiment, a beam of light (say, a laser) is directed at a plate with two holes (see Figure 9-2). The light is then observed on a screen behind this plate. The wave properties in light cause these waves passing through the two slits an interference, producing bands of various brightness on the rear screen; this wouldn't happen if purely particle-based physics were at play (see Figure 9-3). However, each individual photon still (i.e., light particle) passes through a single slit like it would in classical particle physics instead of both holes. This seems to be the behavior with other types of particles as well, including electrons. Again, larger entities, such as molecules, also exhibit this behavior in the experiment.

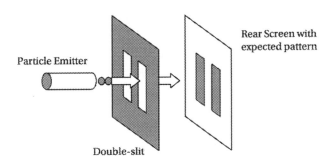

Figure 9-2. The basic setup of a double-slit experiment representing the expected result

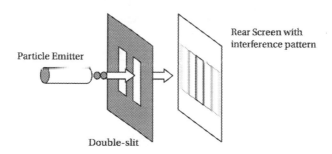

Figure 9-3. *The basic setup of a double-slit experiment with the actual result*

Waves, Phase, and Quantum Coherence/ Decoherence

As you may have already gathered, in quantum mechanics particles are described as *wave functions*. These are probabilistic mathematical representations of quantum states. A definite phase relation between these waves/quantum states is called *coherence*. This is a necessary attribute in quantum computing and all of its related applications.

As a reminder, a *wave* refers to a time-dependent quantity set in a physical or theoretical space. Waves in motion carry energy. All matter operates in waves. Mechanical waves need a medium to operate in (e.g., water or sand), whereas electromagnetic waves (e.g., light) can operate in a vacuum. A *phase* describes the relationship between waves (see Figure 9-4); out-of-phase waves are usually representative of some type of distortion, asymmetry, or (in the quantum realm) decoherence.

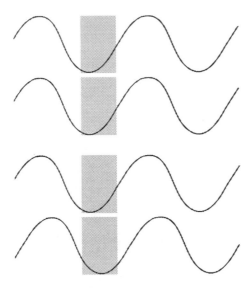

Figure 9-4. *Phase relation visualized. The above two waves are in phase, and below they're out of phase*

Now, in a completely isolated system a quantum coherence would in theory last forever. Measuring parts of such a system without interfering with its coherence is unfortunately impossible. With more measurement, more *decoherence* would be introduced into a quantum system. Therefore, not even quantum mechanisms are impervious to the potentially detrimental effects of time and measurement; this vulnerability is to a degree shared with classical physics and their applications when it comes to their eventual losses of energy.

The Planck Constant and Planck Units

Presented to the world by Nobel Prize–winning physicist **Max Planck** (1858–1947), Planck units are used for measurements on the smallest scale in physics. There are five base units and a plethora of derived ones; we'll only go through the former.

Now it's time to glance at the most relevant Planck units in some detail to give you an understanding of why they are crucial to quantum mechanics. Planck also formulated an important physics constant which we'll discuss first. Prepare yourself for an onslaught of Planck!

The Planck Constant

The *Planck's constant* defines the amount of energy a photon (i.e., an elementary light particle) can carry; it defines the smallest unit for energy. These constants are whole number multiples of base number labeled *h*. This means particles vibrate at, say, base *h* or *4h*, but not *2.4h* or *1.6h*.

The exact value of the Planck constant has been refined and updated over the decades. As of 2019, the value of this constant was fixed at **6.62607015x10^{-34} Joule seconds** according to the *National Institute of Standards and Technology (NIST)*.

I. Planck Length

The unit used to measure the distance light travels during one unit of Planck time is known as the *Planck length*. It's defined using three fundamental constants of physics, namely, the speed of light in a vacuum, Newton's gravitational constant, and the previously mentioned Planck constant.

II. Planck Time

You've probably heard of milliseconds (1/1000 sec) and maybe even of microseconds (1/1000 000 sec). While these are both formidably small increments of time, none is mightier (or more minuscule) than *Planck time*. This unit represents the smallest useful piece of time we're aware of at approximately 10^{-43} seconds; this is the time it takes for a photon to travel at light speed for the length of one *Planck length*.

    Planck time's usefulness is derived from the fact that smaller time units may bear little to no relevance in our study of the universe. This unit is simply small enough to allow us to observe and explain the behavior of quantum entities accurately.

The age of the universe is estimated to be 8×10^{60} in Planck time or approximately 13.8 billion years. This was inferred by studying the oldest objects in the universe and measuring the rate of its expansion. What sucks is even after all this time there are very few reliable observations of flying cars on planet Earth.

III. Planck Temperature

Being the polar opposite of *absolute zero* (e.g., zero kelvins, or −273.15° Celsius), the *Planck temperature* represents the known upper limit of temperature. This stands at 10^{32} kelvins or about one decillion (or 1,42 0,000,000,000,000,000,000,000,000,000,000) degrees of Celsius. There are no theories for matter's behavior above the Planck temperature. Such a set of circumstances would make gravity as potent as any of the four fundamental forces (see "The Standard Model" in this chapter). To describe such settings, a widely accepted quantum theory of gravity would be needed, and as of 2020, one doesn't exist.

IV. Planck Charge

The unit denoting electric charge of particles in the Planck system is known as the *Planck charge*. This unit is a measurement of wave amplitude at the first wavelength in an electron's core when energy is not used for *spin* (see section on "Atoms and Sub-atomic Particles" in this chapter). The longitudinal wave length is reduced when energy is used for spin.

V. Planck Mass

As you may have guessed, the *Planck mass* represents a unit of mass in the Planck system; it stands at roughly 21.7647 micrograms. To the naked human eye, this represents a grain of sand, but by sub-atomic standards, this is a rather large unit. This is because gravity is a relatively weak force in the universe, mostly exerting its effects on larger masses.

Quantum Entanglement

One of the most curious (and useful, from an engineering point of view) properties of sub-atomic particles is known as *quantum entanglement*. These particles can be made to share their quantum states, even when they are physically far apart. This is one phenomenon that is firmly rooted in modern physics and in some conflict with classical mechanics.

Entangled particles are a valuable resource for several applications. Currently, quantum entanglement has been demonstrated to work for distances up to 1200 kilometers. A satellite successfully relayed two entangled photons to ground stations in 2017 (Juan, Yuan, Yu-Huai et al., 2017).

As mentioned in previous chapters, this feature of the quantum world alone will revolutionize secure data transmission. Cryptography aside, quantum entanglement offers other, rather wild applications in the future such as teleportation (i.e., instant travel).

And Now We Need to Talk About Cats

Being somewhat of the star topic of Chapter 8, *superposition* must be a concept of some familiarity to you by now. To recap, elemental particles in the sub-atomic realm can occupy more than one state at a given time. This works great for cryptography in the near future and it naturally has several other implications.

Now, in case you are not familiar with it, *Schrödinger's cat* is an oft-told thought experiment demonstrating superposition devised by Nobel Prize–winning physicist **Erwin Schrödinger** in 1935. This is one of these things some scientists might appreciate you knowing.

Picture a cat put in a closed box for exactly one hour. A rather devious set of props are also contained within said box: a Geiger counter with radioactive particles and a jar of poison. Should the particles decay within an hour, a hammer will fall down to break the jar and release the poison killing the cat. Otherwise, the feline will be fine. So, for one hour, the said mammal is considered simultaneously dead and alive.

In Closing

After finishing this chapter, you will have learned the following:

- What classical and modern physics refer to, including the related main scientific theories

- The basics of the four fundamental forces

- What the main components of a black hole are

- Which kinds of elementary particles exist and what their main qualities are, including the story and importance of the Higgs boson

- The essentials of Max Planck's natural units

- What the double-slit experiment and Schrödinger's cat refers to

In the next chapter we'll take a few back steps and return to the world of cryptography, now armed to our molars with new knowledge.

References

Newburgh, Ronald. 2001. *Phys. Educ.* https://doi.org/10.1088/0031-9120/36/3/304

Hopkins, P. F., Hernquist, L., & Cox, T. J. et al. *A Unified, Merger-driven Model of the Origin of Starbursts, Quasars, the Cosmic X-Ray Background, Supermassive Black Holes, and Galaxy Spheroids,* The Astrophysical Journal Supplement Series, Vol. 163, 2006

Klesman, Alison. *What are primordial black holes?* Astronomy Magazine, 2019.

Sholtis, Sam. *Beyond the black hole singularity,* Penn State Science Journal, Summer 2019

Samanta-Laughton, Manjir. *Punk Science: Inside the Mind of God.* O Books, 2006

Racorean, Ovidiu. *Spacetime manipulation of quantum information around rotating black holes. Annals of Physics.* Vol. 398, pp. 254-264, 2018.

Baudis, Laura. *Direct dark matter detection: The next decade. Physics of the Dark Universe,* Vol. 1, issues 1-2, 2012.

Juan Yin, Yuan Cao, Yu-Huai Li et.al. *Science* 16 Jun 2017: Vol. 356, Issue 6343, pp. 1140-1144

CHAPTER 10

Quantum Information Science 101

The majority of this chapter will be devoted to logic-related side of quantum-based computing in the form of logic gates and related concepts. The four main quantum computing models will also be covered, namely, quantum gate arrays, one-way quantum computers, adiabatic quantum systems, and topological quantum computers. While not exactly mainstream right now, quantum devices are well on their way. Absorb this chapter well and you will stay ahead of the trajectory in these matters; you're reading about the near future with all its implications for you and/ or your organization after all.

Logic Gates

To gain a better understanding of the various concepts and possibilities quantum-based computing offers, we should visit some areas of classical computing first. Let's take a solid gander at *logic gates*. While originating firmly in the era of classical computing, they are a relevant concept in the world of quantum computing as well.

© Robert Ciesla 2020
R. Ciesla, *Encryption for Organizations and Individuals*,
https://doi.org/10.1007/978-1-4842-6056-2_10

Now, a classical logic gate is a construct which accepts binary data; that is information consisting of either ones or zeros (or trues or falses, or perhaps smoking and nonsmoking, you name it). After some processing, a gate outputs a single binary result (e.g., smoking or nonsmoking). These functions consisting of only two types of elements for both the input and the output are known as *Boolean functions*.

You might remember the **exclusive OR (XOR)** function from Chapter 3. It's the logical operation extensively used in several cryptographic algorithms, including the indomitable AES.

And what is the big deal about these logic gates? Basically, they are the building blocks of any electronic device. Typically, voltage is fed into a circuit, and as it traverses through logic gates, a variety of different things can occur. A simple implementation of logic gates can be found in electronic door buzzers. Although, say, microprocessors are much more complex, these two types of devices still share some fundamental similarities. A *central processing unit (CPU)* in a modern computer has up to several billion logic gates, in the form of *transistors*, built-in. A transistor refers to an electronic component which can either be used to amplify signals or to act as a gate.

Now, XOR aside, there are several logical operations most electronic devices, from digital watches to the latest gaming console, utilize. See Table 10-1 for a demonstration of how the different logical operators work on binary data.

Table 10-1. *Some common logical operations on binary data*

Operation and Symbol		Input A	Input B	Output /Result
Exclusive OR (XOR)	$A \oplus B$	0	0	0
		0	1	1
		1	0	1
		1	1	0
OR	$A \vee B$	0	0	0
		0	1	1
		1	0	1
		1	1	1
Not OR (NOR)	$A \downarrow B$	0	0	1
		0	1	0
		1	0	0
		1	1	0
Exclusive Not OR (XNOR)	$A \odot B$	0	0	1
		0	1	0
		1	0	0
		1	1	1
AND	$A \cdot B$	0	0	0
		0	1	0
		1	0	0
		1	1	1
Not AND (NAND)	$A \uparrow B$	0	0	1
		0	1	1
		1	0	1
		1	1	0

As a reminder, although logic gates have their origins in classical computing, they are still applicable in quantum-based computers as you will learn later in this chapter.

Quantum Computer Says No: Error Correction

All devices break down. The job of error correction is to keep a system running, even when a data-related crash might be in progress. Error correction is damage management; instead of data loss and total system failure, the computation might just slow down a little. This key property is called *fault tolerance*. Current-generation computers, especially in the professional segment, tend to be well catered for in this respect. Since quantum computers are an emerging technology, the same level of fault tolerance for these types of devices is still being discovered – and already with some success. These mostly experimental techniques constitute a field called *quantum error correction (QEC)*. We'll now delve a little into this fascinating, emerging science.

One of the biggest gremlins for quantum computers comes in the form of *decoherence*. Basically this refers to the scenario in which quantum effects, such as superposition and entanglement, are compromised by intrusions by outside forces. A quantum-based system will invariably experience some entanglement between qubits and their surroundings. To a degree, qubits will undergo unwanted phase variance making accurate calculations more challenging or impossible. Reducing decoherence is one of the key issues addressed by emerging quantum error correction. So far, technologies like high magnetic fields have been successfully used to counter decoherence. Magnets to the rescue!

The much-researched field of error correction in the realm of classical bits often relies on redundancy, that is, making multiple copies of information. Technology called *error correction code (ECC)*, found in many devices and professional computer components, makes great use of redundancy. In the nonclassical domain, the property of entanglement can be used in place of copying quantum information.

Now, another class of concepts you should be aware of are the *no-go theorems*. These represent events in physics which are not deemed possible, as far as we currently know. There are several of these theorems in quantum physics and they can be summed up as follows:

- The *no-cloning theorem* was discovered by physicist *James Park* in 1970. It states that it's simply not possible to duplicate an arbitrary unknown quantum state.

- The *no-deleting theorem* is a time-reversed companion to the previous theorem. It states that when presented with two identical quantum states, you cannot delete one of them. Again, this is a phenomenon not known in classical computing, where copying and deleting binary data is as trivial as it gets. Physicists *Arun K. Pati* and *Samuel L. Braunstein* proved the no-deleting theorem.

- The *no-teleportation theorem* states that arbitrary quantum states can't (a) be converted into classical bits and (b) re-created using classical bits. This theorem is named after the "teleportation" of quantum states into classical binary data; it has very little to do with *quantum teleportation*, which is a separate topic altogether.

- The *no-communication theorem* is another no-go theorem which states that when measuring quantum states, no sharing of information using classical bits can occur between different observers of these events.

213

A *theorem* is a non-self-evident mathematical statement that has been proven to be true. This concept is not synonymous with a *theory*, which refers to a set of ideas used to explain a phenomenon. You do not need actual proof to devise a theory, but it's mandatory in the case of theorems. A solid theory, however, does need ample amounts of supporting evidence.

In the light of all these no-go theorems, there are a variety of issues in quantum error correction. Copying data, for one, is not an option. However, quantum data can be spread between groups of qubits. A promising approach in mitigating the issue is to be found in *logical qubits*. These are basically collections of qubits serving as a single unit. This provides a more robust and safeguarded level of processing data in a quantum computer.

The previously discussed ECC uses the implementation of *repetition code* rather extensively. Basically the technique entails resending data over a channel until intact data makes it to the intended receiver. Classical ECC repetition code doesn't work with qubits, due to the no-cloning theorem. However, quantum computers can sidestep this limitation with several unique approaches and enjoy a reasonable level of fault tolerance.

One of the mightiest ways to provide sturdy quantum error correction is known as *Shor Code* named after professor of applied mathematics *Peter Shor* at the *Massachusetts Institute of Technology*. A Shor Code circuit takes one logical qubit consisting of nine actual qubits. The approach can correct any arbitrary errors occurring in a single qubit.

As mighty as the Shor Code is, there are other types of error-correcting approaches in the quantum realm. Canadian physicist *Raymond Laflamme* and his team developed a highly optimized code in which an initial quantum state is processed with four extra qubits in state $|0\rangle$, therefore only requiring a total of five qubit units. The method is known as *Perfect Quantum Error Correcting Code* (Laflamme et al. 1996).

Four Approaches to Quantum Computing

We'll now go into detail about some of the general approaches to quantum computing. There is no single "correct" or mainstream approach yet as this technology is still in a state of growth.

I. Quantum Gate Array (Quantum Circuit)

A *quantum gate* is a basic quantum circuit operating with a small number of qubits. A sequence of these gates constitutes an approach called a *quantum gate array*. This is often also referred to as a *quantum circuit*.

A quantum gate array uses several attributes of quantum mechanics, such as superposition and entanglement, to reach a level of impressive computational processing power. While being more effective, the approach of quantum gate arrays was mostly designed to imitate the logic gates used in classical computing (Delgado, 2017).

There is one major difference between classical- and quantum-based gates; the latter offer a great degree of reversibility. After bits are done passing through arrays of classical logic gates, they often lose their original form for good, usually turning into heat energy. In the quantum realm, thanks to the wonders of entanglement, you are likely to be able to reverse the operations and restore things to their original states. Next, we'll explore some of the most common logical operators found in quantum circuits. See Table 10-2 for a rundown.

Table 10-2. *Some common quantum logic gates, their symbols, and matrix representations. Imaginary units (donated with **i**) form some of these matrices, which are known as complex matrices.*

Gate	Circuit Symbol(s)	Matrix Representation
Pauli-X	$\boxed{X}$ $\oplus$	$X = \begin{pmatrix} 0 & 1 \\ 1 & 0 \end{pmatrix}$
Pauli-Y	$\boxed{Y}$	$Y = \begin{pmatrix} 0 & -i \\ i & 0 \end{pmatrix}$
Pauli-Z	$\boxed{Z}$	$Z = \begin{pmatrix} 1 & 0 \\ 0 & -1 \end{pmatrix}$
Hadamard	$\boxed{H}$	$H = \dfrac{1}{\sqrt{2}} \begin{pmatrix} 1 & 1 \\ 1 & -1 \end{pmatrix}$
Swap		$SWAP = \begin{pmatrix} 1 & 0 & 0 & 0 \\ 0 & 0 & 1 & 0 \\ 0 & 1 & 0 & 0 \\ 0 & 0 & 0 & 1 \end{pmatrix}$
$\sqrt{Swap}$		$\sqrt{SWAP} = \begin{pmatrix} 1 & 0 & 0 & 0 \\ 0 & \frac{1}{2}(1+i) & \frac{1}{2}(1-i) & 0 \\ 0 & \frac{1}{2}(1-i) & \frac{1}{2}(1+i) & 0 \\ 0 & 0 & 0 & 1 \end{pmatrix}$

Universal Quantum Gates

A set of quantum-based gates to which any more complicated operations can be reduced to constitutes the category of *universal quantum gates*. While quantum computing offers in theory an infinite set of gates to work with, all known quantum operations can be approximated by a sequence of gates from a finite set. The *controlled NOT (CNOT)* gate is a universal quantum gate, to name just one.

Universal logic gates aren't naturally only found in the world of quantum mechanics. Some are based in classical computing, while others work with both classical binary data and qubits.

The *Fredkin gate (CSWAP)*, named after computer scientist *Edward Fredkin*, is a universal gate used in both classical and quantum computing. We'll discuss this type of logic gate in more detail later in the chapter.

Now, all quantum gates are reversible, but this goes for only some in the classical binary world. In classical computing, NAND, NOR, and the *Toffoli gate (CCNOT)* represent often-used universal logic gates.

The Toffoli gate is in fact a reversible gate which means that any reversible logic gate can be created with this type of construct. By implementing a Toffoli gate in an environment with logic gates specific to the quantum realm, this gate can also work as a universal quantum gate.

Unitary and Permutation Matrices

A *unitary matrix* is basically a square matrix with a *conjugate transpose* which is also its inverse. This transpose is done by simply flipping a matrix on its head and then discovering its *complex conjugate*. Now, a complex conjugate of a number is a value with an equal real part and imaginary part, the same magnitude, but it has the opposite sign. For example, the complex conjugate of *A+iB* is *A-iB*.

A unitary matrix with its rows and columns consisting of all zeros and a single one is called *a permutation matrix (P)*. In other words, each of these rows and columns must have a total value of one. In quantum physics single-qubit logical gates, such as the Pauli gates, discussed soon, can be represented by a simple 2 x 2 matrix.

Later in the chapter we'll come across several of these permutation matrices as quantum logic gates represent this type of mathematical object; stay tuned!

All Things Eigen

When studying fields related to quantum mechanics, you will undoubtedly come across a plethora of concepts will the prefix of *eigen*. We'll now cover the basics of what these terms actually refer to.

Any set of data points can be deconstructed into *eigenvalues*, which have a corresponding *eigenvector*. An eigenvector is basically a vector whose direction remains unchanged after a linear transformation. Now, an eigenvalue generally tells us the amount of variance a dataset has when traversing on an eigenvector. In a geometrical context, an eigenvector points in a direction in which it is resized by a transformation; the associated eigenvalue provides the factor with which the vector is stretched by. See Figure 10-1 for a simple visual demonstration of this.

As a refresher, a *linear transformation* is a function from a vector space into another vector space in which both spaces share the underlying linear structure. The process is also called *linear mapping*. A vector space is a collection of vectors, added together and often multiplied (i.e., scaled) by numbers known as *scalars*.

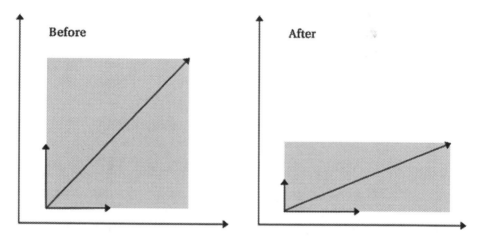

Figure 10-1. *A visual demonstration of an eigenvector. The vector directions remain the same after transformation*

Eigenvectors and eigenvalues have several important applications in computing in general, including facial recognition and many other types of (semi-)automized analysis. Several search engines, including *Google*, use eigenvalues and eigenvectors to provide search results as accurately as possible.

An *eigenstate* of some operator is a quantum state which, upon measurement, will yield a result; it basically refers to the previously discussed phenomenon of superposition.

Finally, there's the *eigenfunction*. This refers to a set of independent functions used to provide a solution to a *differential equation* (basically, these types of equations are there to help us understand how things change). In quantum mechanics, one of the most important *partial differential equations* is *Schrödinger's equation*, which describes wave functions, that is, quantum states. You might remember the name from the previous chapter. With his equation, Schrödinger combined classical mechanics with quantum-based physics to explain the particle/wave duality found in the sub-atomic realm.

Oh, and, in case you're wondering, *eigen* comes from German and roughly translated means *proper*.

Pauli Gates

An important category of logical operators in the quantum world are known as the *Pauli gates*, named after the Austrian theoretical physicist *Wolfgang Pauli (1900–1958)*. You might remember the Bloch sphere representation of qubits we discussed in the previous chapters; Pauli gates rotate a qubit in its three axes of x, y, and z.

These operators are simply called Pauli-X, Pauli-Y, and Pauli-Z. Of these, the Pauli-X gate is the quantum equivalent of the classical NOT operator: it reverses the (spin-)state of a particle switching spin-up to spin-down or vice versa.

The Hadamard Gate

A quantum logic gate which takes a qubit's definite state (i.e., 0 or 1) and returns it back to superposition is known as the *Hadamard gate*, named after French mathematician *Jacques Hadamard (1865–1963)*.

The Swap Gates

As its name suggests, the *swap gate* simply switches two qubits around a logical circuit. This gate is often stylized in all capitals, that is, "SWAP". Another type of swap gate, the *square root of swap gate*, only performs its operations half-way. Any multiple-qubit quantum gates can be constructed by combining the square root of swap with single-qubit gates.

Figure 10-2 shows the layout of a simple quantum circuit. The top state fed into the system is a zero. It is input into a Hadamard gate, throwing the value into superposition (the 50/50 state). The next state is again a zero; however, it swaps position with the first state. The last line shows again a value of zero, this time entering a Pauli-X gate (i.e., a quantum NOT operator) transforming it into a definite one/On.

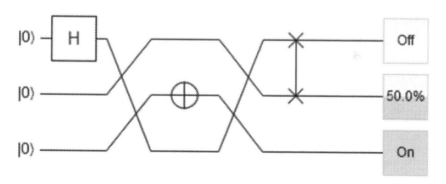

Figure 10-2. *A simple quantum circuit demonstrating the Hadamard, Pauli-X, and SWAP gates*

Toffoli and Fredkin Gates

A special mention belongs to the *Toffoli gate* which, like we discussed, serves as a reversible universal gate. We'll now go into more detail on this magnificent bit manipulator. Also described as the *controlled-controlled-not (CCNOT) gate*, this gate was invented by professor *Tommaso Toffoli* in 1980. A Toffoli gate was successfully first implemented in practice in 2009 at the University of Innsbruck, Austria.

Now, the Toffoli has 3-bit inputs and outputs; if the first two bits are both set to 1, it inverts the third bit; otherwise, all bits stay the same. In its quantum version, five two-qubit quantum gates are required to run a Toffoli gate. A quantum-based Toffoli gate is essentially a quantum/reversible version of the classical AND gate (see Table 10-3).

Table 10-3. *The Toffoli and Fredkin gate circuit symbols and their matrix representations*

Gate	Circuit Symbol(s)	Matrix Representation
Toffoli		$CCNOT = \begin{bmatrix} 1 & 0 & 0 & 0 & 0 & 0 & 0 & 0 \\ 0 & 1 & 0 & 0 & 0 & 0 & 0 & 0 \\ 0 & 0 & 1 & 0 & 0 & 0 & 0 & 0 \\ 0 & 0 & 0 & 1 & 0 & 0 & 0 & 0 \\ 0 & 0 & 0 & 0 & 1 & 0 & 0 & 0 \\ 0 & 0 & 0 & 0 & 0 & 1 & 0 & 0 \\ 0 & 0 & 0 & 0 & 0 & 0 & 0 & 1 \\ 0 & 0 & 0 & 0 & 0 & 0 & 1 & 0 \end{bmatrix}$
Fredkin		$CSWAP = \begin{bmatrix} 1 & 0 & 0 & 0 & 0 & 0 & 0 & 0 \\ 0 & 1 & 0 & 0 & 0 & 0 & 0 & 0 \\ 0 & 0 & 1 & 0 & 0 & 0 & 0 & 0 \\ 0 & 0 & 0 & 1 & 0 & 0 & 0 & 0 \\ 0 & 0 & 0 & 0 & 1 & 0 & 0 & 0 \\ 0 & 0 & 0 & 0 & 0 & 0 & 1 & 0 \\ 0 & 0 & 0 & 0 & 0 & 1 & 0 & 0 \\ 0 & 0 & 0 & 0 & 0 & 0 & 0 & 1 \end{bmatrix}$

The Toffoli gate plays an important role in quantum error correcting; this makes it also important in quantum state initialization, manipulation, and measurement. For these reasons the Toffoli gate has been researched rather thoroughly (Shi 2018).

As discussed previously in the chapter, a *Fredkin gate* is another type of universal logic gate. Often also referred to as the CSWAP gate, it consists of three inputs and outputs. A Fredkin gate swaps the second and third bits only, as long as the first one holds the value of one (1). CSWAP stands for *controlled swap*.

In 2016 researchers from the *University of Queensland* and the *Griffith University* completed a quantum Fredkin gate using entangled photons (i.e., light particles) to swap qubits. This type of Fredkin gate was a major step in facilitating quantum computing as it allows the building of large quantum circuits consisting of only a few types of logic gates (Patel, Ho, Ferreytol et al. 2016).

II. The Topological Quantum Computer

A quantum system using two-dimensional quasiparticles known as *anyons* is called a *topological quantum computer.*

Now, an anyon is a particle found in two-dimensional spaces only with less restrictions than, say, a boson (as discussed in the previous chapter). Contrary to what you might think, there are two-dimensional spaces embedded in our mostly three-dimensional understanding of the world. In physics these are referred to as *membranes* or *surfaces.*

A topological quantum computer uses these two-dimensional anyons to create *braids.* Braids are abstract mathematical objects represented as parallel and/or interconnected lines whose points of origin and end points are fixed (see Figure 10-3).

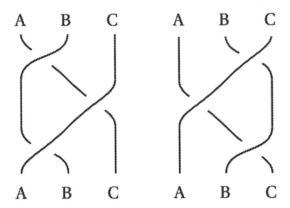

Figure 10-3. *Example braid charts*

Braids operate in three-dimensional space-time to form logic gates applicable to quantum information science. A topological quantum computer, once actually constructed, would offer robust error-correcting capabilities in the quantum realm. An error-correcting method known as *toric code* is an inherent part of any topological computer.

III. The Adiabatic Quantum Computer (AQC)

The *adiabatic theorem* is an important concept in quantum physics. It states that a quantum system gradually subjected to external forces adapts to them, where as a sudden exertion of external forces tends to keep the quantum probabilities intact. The phenomenon was first described by physicists *Max Born* and *Vladimir Fock* in 1928.

A *Hamiltonian (H)* in quantum physics is an operator used to represent the total amount of energy in a system. This function was named after *William R. Hamilton (1805–1865)*, an Irish mathematician who successfully reformulated Newtonian mechanics through his work.

The adiabatic approach uses time-dependent smoothly interpolating Hamiltonians. If this Hamiltonian oscillates slowly enough, the adiabatic theorem makes sure that a quantum measurement with this type of system will be accurate.

It has been postulated that an adiabatic quantum computer would offer the greatest degree of quantum error correction for the time being; such a system is likely to be highly resistant against quantum decoherence, for one (Childs, Farhi, Preskill 2001).

IV. One-Way Quantum Computer

A *one-way quantum computer* uses the phenomenon of quantum entanglement (familiar from Chapter 9) in the form of *cluster states*; these are groups of highly entangled qubits. This approach gets its name from the fact that each cluster state is destroyed upon measurement. One-way quantum computers can utilize quantum logic gates in the preparation of each cluster state (Raussendorf, Briegel 2001).

One-way quantum computers are in fact nonreversible in their calculations. The order and choices of measurements define the computed algorithm to be used (Nature 2005). Any practical implementations of a one-way quantum computer must also implement a high degree of fault tolerance as quantum noise and decoherence are to be expected.

In Closing

After finishing this chapter, you will have learned the following:

- What logic gates are and how they relate to quantum computers

- The main no-go theorems of quantum computing when it comes to data duplication and deletion

- What quantum error correction (QEC) refers to

- The four main approaches of quantum computing

- The most common logical operators in classical and quantum computing

In the next chapter we'll enter the fray of quantum encryption in full force. And armed with all of this new knowledge, it'll indubitably turn out to be a winning fight for you, dear reader.

References

Perfect Quantum Error Correcting Code. Raymond Laflamme, Cesar Miquel, Juan Pablo Paz, and Wojciech Hubert Zurek. Phys. Rev. Lett. 77, 198 (1996).

F. Delgado 2017 J. Phys.: Conf. Ser. 839 012014

Shi, Xiao-Feng. "Deutsch, Toffoli, and Cnot Gates via Rydberg Blockade of Neutral Atoms." Physical Review Applied 9.5 (2018).

Patel, Ho, Ferreytol et al. Science Advances, 2016: Vol. 2, no. 3, e1501531. DOI: 10.1126/sciadv.1501531 https://advances.sciencemag.org/content/2/3/e1501531

Childs, Farhi, Preskill 2001. *Robustness of adiabatic quantum computation.* Physical Review A 65.1

Raussendorf, Briegel 2001. *A One-Way Quantum Computer.* Phys. Rev. Lett. 86, 5188

Nature volume 434, pages 169–176 (2005)

CHAPTER 11

Quantum Cryptography

In this chapter we'll explore more of some of the most essential components of quantum-based cryptography, including the grandparent of quantum key distribution protocols, the formidable *BB84*. You'll see some familiar concepts and names, but you will probably also encounter several new ideas.

On Quantum Key Distribution (QKD)

We'll now probe into some of the most important concepts related to quantum cryptography, including *quantum key distribution (QKD)*. Do note that QKD is not the same as quantum encryption; it is instead a very effective auxiliary technique for securing keys/passwords. Current implementations of QKD are to be used in tandem with well-established classical algorithms, such as the AES.

A number of transmission protocols exist for QKD. We'll next discuss some of these protocols in detail.

© Robert Ciesla 2020
R. Ciesla, *Encryption for Organizations and Individuals*,
https://doi.org/10.1007/978-1-4842-6056-2_11

Let's Go with Light

Quantum communications can be implemented using several varieties of quantum particles, including ions, atoms, and light (i.e., photons). Out of these, unit light tends to interact with matter to the smallest degree as photons are massless. This makes photons the optimal choice of transfer unit when it comes to tackling the issue of decoherence (as discussed in Chapter 10). Light, however, does sometimes disperse over time; a few of those important photons may never arrive at their intended destination. How these losses affect quantum communications is largely dependent on which protocol is being used (Scarani et al. 2009).

BB84

Developed all the way back in 1984 by *Charles Bennett* and *Gilles Brassard*, the *BB84* was the first cryptographic protocol that allowed legitimate parties to detect eavesdropping during message transmission. It uses Heisenberg's uncertainty principle, which as you might remember from Chapter 9 states that quantum-based data can't be measured without disturbing it.

The information sent using BB84 is encoded in the polarization of photons. Polarization refers to the geometrical orientation of the oscillations in (light) waves; the property is expressed in degrees, for example, 90° (see Figure 11-1). Optical fiber is a typical carrier medium for this approach.

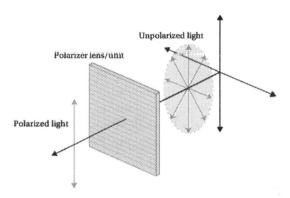

Figure 11-1. *The oscillation patterns of photons can be altered using polarizer devices*

Polarization can be performed either on a rectilinear or diagonal basis in BB84 (see Figure 11-2). The sender side chooses which basis/approach to use for each bit and informs the receiver; this stage is called *key sifting*. Often a nonsecure conventional channel of communication is used with the BB84 for negotiation and sifting purposes.

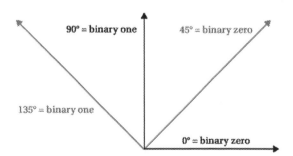

Figure 11-2. *Bits can be encoded in the polarization states of a photon in the BB84 protocol. The black arrows denote the rectilinear basis*

Now, let's do some key sifting and simulate a small quantum transmission between two parties, Adramicia-Alphonsine and Biniyaamzawed. Whenever these two share bases and measurements, they form parts of the secret key (see Table 11-1).

Table 11-1. *A small sifted key. The plus sign denotes a rectilinear basis, while X refers to the diagonal one*

Adramicia-Alphonsine's bit	1	1	0	0	0	1	1	1
Adramicia-Alphonsine's basis	+	X	+	X	X	+	X	+
Adramicia-Alphonsine's polarization	90°	45°	0°	135°	45°	90°	45°	0°
Biniyaamzawed's basis	+	X	+	X	+	X	+	+
Biniyaamzawed's measurement	90°	45°	90°	135°	90°	45°	0°	0°
Shared bits (i.e., the secret password/key)	1	1		0				1

Key sifting is often performed on a more or less open channel such as the Internet. Although it might sound risky, malicious actors cannot often use sifting-related communications to gain information on any keys/passwords transmitted using QKD.

The no-cloning theorem (see Chapter 10) guarantees information can't be duplicated in this realm. Also, any eavesdropping on channels using the BB84 protocol will result in an increased rate of quantum errors; this will let the legitimate parties know they are being spied upon.

B92

Developed by Charles Bennett of BB84 fame, the *B92* is basically an optimized version of his previous protocol. Instead of four polarized states, the B92 offers just two (Ouchao, Jakimi 2018). Transmission of the basis (i.e., rectilinear or diagonal) used in the sifting stage is also not needed in B92. While easier to implement than the BB84, the newer protocol is thought to be less secure.

The Six-State Protocol (SSP)

Based on BB84, the *six-state protocol* operates on six states of polarization (on three orthogonal bases), instead of the four found in BB84 (see Figure 11-3). Eavesdropping on an implementation of the SSP produces a high rate of error, making unmasking malicious actors very effective. Although this approach is among the most secure protocols, it carries with it additional risks of data loss.

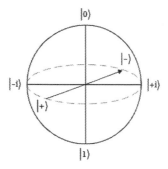

Figure 11-3. *The three bases and six states of polarization of the SSP represented with a Bloch sphere*

The Ekert Protocol (E91)

The *Ekert protocol* uses quantum entanglement with a central source between two parties to transmit messages simultaneously; a currently known practical source could be a satellite in orbit. The photons used in the protocol are entangled and assigned with randomized polarization.

The *Einstein–Podolsky–Rosen paradox (EPR paradox)* is a thought experiment devised in 1935 basically stating that quantum mechanics were in fact considered an incomplete paradigm. The quantum properties of entanglement and superposition in particular were thought to be in conflict with classical physics. The Ekert protocol actually provides a functional framework for putting the theoretical physics outlined in the EPR paradox into practice (Ilic 2007).

Continuous-Variable (CV) Protocols

The previously introduced protocols have been *discrete variable* in nature in which information is carried by single, or entangled, photons. A *continuous-variable (CV) protocol* is a different approach in which amplitudes, instead of individual photons, are measured. The photon counter units in discrete-variable protocols slow down the proceedings a tad and are not needed with continuous-variable protocols. Although generally faster during operation, CV protocols tend to produce more errors (Scarani et al. 2009).

Shor's (Factoring) Algorithm

Some encryption schemes previously thought of as impenetrable are meeting their matches. One such scenario unfolded when *Peter Shor's factoring algorithm* emerged in 1994, which is bad news for public-key cryptographic approaches such as the RSA. Shor's algorithm was devised to discover prime factors of arbitrary numbers.

In practice, Shor's algorithm consists of two phases; the first of which may be performed on a classical computer. In 2001 IBM built a seven-qubit quantum computer and with it successfully demonstrated the second part of Shor's algorithm.

Now, are algorithms like the RSA in peril? Not really. For its 2048-bit variety at least, we would need a quantum computer of several hundred qubits to make the wait palatable. In addition, even if we managed to create such a computer, the issue of decoherence remains; as discussed in the previous chapter, qubits eventually lose their luster with their quantum properties. And we can forget about a classical supercomputer working on cracking the RSA with its several trillion year time frame.

Quantum Coin Flipping

Sometimes you can't be sure that the receiving end of quantum communications is the intended one. *Quantum coin flipping* is a protocol for two parties who do not trust each other. The technique is being researched for secure authentication (i.e., fingerprinting) purposes as some stages in a typical QKD process involve nonsecure channels of communication. An approach where quantum coin flipping is executed after QKD is performed has been proposed; this would thwart most attempts at a man-in-the-middle attack (Rass et al. 2009).

In Closing

After finishing this chapter, you will have learned the following:

- Which established protocols exist for *quantum key distribution (QKD)*, in particular the *BB84* and the basics of its workings

- What *key sifting* means

- The significance of *Shor's algorithm* and *quantum coin flipping*

In the next chapter we'll delve much deeper into the fascinating theme of quantum-based cryptography. There are still many concepts left to unearth in quantum key distribution alone, for one.

References

B. Ouchao, A. Jakimi. International Journal of Advanced Engineering, Management and Science, June 2018. Performance Evaluation of Secure Key Distribution Based on the B92 Protocol.

Scarani, Bechmann-Pasquinucci et al. Rev.Mod.Phys. 81, 2009. The Security of Practical Quantum Key Distribution.

Ilic, Nikolina J. Phy 334, 2007. The Ekert Protocol.

S. Rass, P. Schartner, M. Greiler. 2009 IEEE International Conference on Communications. Quantum Coin-Flipping-Based Authentication.

CHAPTER 12

Quantum Key Distribution Under Attack

In this chapter we'll continue on the emerging science of quantum
key distribution (QKD). This is a key technology and will undoubtedly
play a big part in many a person's life in the near future. The concepts
introduced in the last chapter will be greatly expanded upon, including the
hardware side of things. But first, we'll cover various types of QKD-focused
cryptographic attacks as these unfortunately will be an issue.

Breaking QKD

Although representative of the next generation of computing, QKD is
not impervious to malicious activities. Some of these attack vectors
will resemble those found in classical computing. However, some
are only implementable in the world of quantum cryptography. The
attacks described next mostly target the BB84 protocol and its many
derivatives.

© Robert Ciesla 2020
R. Ciesla, *Encryption for Organizations and Individuals*,
https://doi.org/10.1007/978-1-4842-6056-2_12

Photon Number Splitting (PNS)

Using the BB84 protocol, Alice would be ideally sending Bob a single photon at a time. However, due to the limitations of creating single photons under most circumstances, sometimes more than one photon is sent during transmission with BB84. This paves the way for *photon number splitting*. In this attack, Eve the eavesdropper can intercept some photons while letting others reach their intended recipient that is, Bob. Due to negligible rates of quantum errors in this attack vector (i.e., photon loss), both legitimate parties will assume to be in transmission with each other only. This leads to a scenario in which Eve knows exactly what Alice is trying to communicate to Bob while remaining completely invisible herself (Zhao, 2018).

A family of protocols free of key sifting has been proposed to provide resistance to photon number splitting (Grazioso & Grosshans 2013). The decoy state protocol, too, offers protection against this variety of attack.

The *decoy state protocol* uses several settings of intensity in the transmitter side. Only one of these settings contains valuable information; the rest are decoys. Only after each transmission is the intended intensity setting revealed. This approach offers good protection against the photon number-splitting attack. The decoy state protocol has been confirmed to work over distances of at least 100 kilometers.

Denial of Service

Instead of flooding a server with requests as is the case in a classical denial-of-service (DoS) attack, in quantum-based settings malicious actors can simply cut fiber optic cords. In the case of unsealed optical quantum transmission devices, blocking the line of sight between these units also does the trick. A quantum DoS is there primarily to disrupt any proceedings and not to gather intelligence.

Trojan Horse

Its name notwithstanding, the *Trojan horse attack* in a quantum context shares very little with its classical counterpart. Instead of a malicious software package, the quantum-based Trojan horse uses the approach of shining a bright beam of light into the quantum channel and examining its back reflections. With only a handful of reflected photons, an eavesdropper can deduce the basis choice of one of the legitimate parties (Nitin et al. 2014).

A Trojan horse attack in the context of QKDs is also known as a *large pulse attack*.

Intercept and Resend (IR)

The *intercept and resend* attack is exactly what it sounds like. An eavesdropper called Eve intercepts photons Alice intends to reach Bob. Eve replaces these photons with another set which she has already measured. Statistically speaking Eve is successful in getting the basis right 50% of the time. In turn Bob is also right 50% in deducing Eve's basis. This results in a detectable error rate of 25% (50% of 50% equals 25%).

A variation of this attack known as the *Intercept and Resend with Faked States (IRFS)* does not focus on guessing any original basis states. Instead Eve's emphasis is on producing pulses of light detectable by Bob. This provides a cover for eavesdropping; Alice and Bob think they are operating with unaltered quantum states, unaware of Eve's influence on the proceedings. This can reveal the full secret key/password without raising alarm via spikes in the quantum error rate (Lizama-Pérez et al. 2016).

Thermal Blinding Attack

Sometimes bright light is all it takes to compromise a QKD-based system. A type of attack known as *thermal blinding* uses continuous-wave illumination and short, bright trigger pulses to manipulate voltages in a quantum circuit. This can reveal the full key/password without raising the qubit error rate, which would under most circumstances raise an alarm. As of 2020, at least the *Clavis2* QKD system has been compromised using this type of attack vector.

Unlike photon counters, *homodyne sensors* may be able to ward off thermal blinding attacks with a considerable rate of success. The technology was also fundamental in demonstrating quantum entanglement.

Man in the Middle

A common type of attack in the classical world, *man in the middle* is also a possibility during any unauthenticated use of QKD. In particular, the calibration phase when establishing a QKD connection may be exposed to this type of attack. By installing a malicious precondition into the signal exchange, an eavesdropper may receive full details on the final key (see Figure 12-1). The BB84 protocol and its derivatives in particular are vulnerable to this attack (Fei & Meng, et al., 2018).

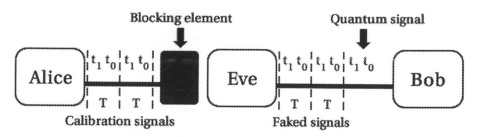

Figure 12-1. *MITM during quantum key distribution. Alice sends calibration signals to Bob only to have them intercepted by Eve, who in turn sends her faked signals to Bob. The **T** denotes a single cycle in a single pulse of photons*

Before quantum key distribution can be initiated, a quantum channel must be established with single-photon detectors. These detectors will be calibrated using a process known as *line length measurement (LLM)*. During a typical LLM, Alice sends calibration signals to the detectors at Bob's disposal. This process includes gauging the channel length and the relative delay between the arrival timing of the pulses. The activation timing of each detector is scanned electronically to discover the timing when the count rates are at maximum (Fei & Meng, et al., 2018).

The receiver, Bob, has photon detectors in place, but he's not aware of Eve the eavesdropper who is actually sending him faked signals. Eve creates discrepancies between the activation timing of the various detectors by replacing the calibration signals with phony ones. These are to contain more than one pulse in each cycle as opposed to the signals sent by Alice, which have one pulse per cycle. The arrival timings of responding signals are denoted as *t0* and *t1* in Figure 12-1. Eve wants to know the activation timing for each detector (i.e., t0 or t1). This can be solved by a *time-shift attack (TSA)* in the beginning of the QKD process during which Eve chooses the arrival timing of signals between t0 and t1 at random (Fei & Meng, et al., 2018).

Now, if this interception of the LLM is successful, Eve will be in complete control over the quantum channel in question while Bob will remain blissfully unaware; this approach constitutes the man-in-the-middle attack in the quantum realm.

The Hardware of QKD

Having looked into potential attack vectors, let's next take a peek at the hardware components a QKD system includes running on the BB84 protocol. The system we are about to explore was based on the work by researchers at *Toshiba Corporate Research Center, Toshiba Research Europe Ltd*, and the *Quantum ICT Laboratory* in Japan.

This system was successfully implemented on a 45-kilometer stretch of a metropolitan telecom network in Tokyo. The QKD transmissions were carried over fiber optic cables (Dixon & Dynes et al., 2017).

Component Breakdown

Next, we'll go through the main components of the Tokyo QKD system; Figures 12-2 and 12-3 show the basic parts of the transmitter and receiver devices the network utilized. These will be discussed in detail.

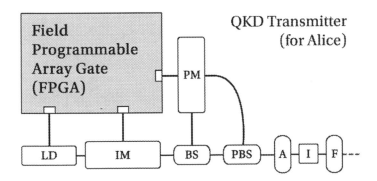

Figure 12-2. *A layout for a secure QKD transmitter device*

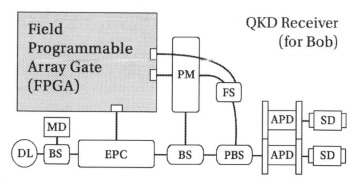

Figure 12-3. A layout for a secure QKD receiver device

The presented design uses *Mach–Zehnder interferometer.* This refers to the technology used to examine relative phase shift variations between two beams derived by splitting light from a single source. Both the transmitter and the receiver devices in the design operate on these principles and contain the necessary hardware to do so.

Field Programmable Array Gate (FPGA)

Found in numerous types of devices, *field programmable array gates* (FPGAs) are semiconductor circuits consisting of a matrix of logic blocks. These are highly configurable units, unlike *application-specific integrated circuits (ASIC)* which are designed for a specific, usually fixed purpose (e.g., CPUs in classical computers). An FPGA is reprogrammable should the need to implement new tasks and/or features arise; it's the perfect prototyping solution. Like you probably noticed from Figures 12-2 and 12-3, an FPGA is a central component to both the receiver and the transmitter device.

In the context of the QKD system presented in this chapter, the FPGAs run at a 1 Gigahertz transmission rate.

Optical Attenuator, Isolator, and Narrow Band Pass Filter

The optical attenuator (A), isolator (I), and narrow band pass filter (F) components work together to reduce the amount of reflected light (see Figure 12-2). In a QKD setting they are responsible for attenuating the photon pulse levels so that information leakage isn't an issue in the context of a quantum Trojan horse attack.

Laser Diode, Intensity Modulator, and Phase Modulator

The *laser diode (LD)* component produces photon pulses, that is, the main units of information in a QKD system (see Figure 12-2). An *intensity modulator (IM)* provides security against photon-splitting attacks by adding decoy states into the stream.

A *phase modulator (PM)* component in this QKD solution can encode four discrete phase values onto the photon pulse; a PM on the receiver's device is then used to decrypt these values.

Beam Splitter and Polarizing Beam Splitter

Beam splitters (BS) are used by the receiver to extract the polarization data of each photon particle. A *polarizing beam splitter (BMS)* ensures that photons travel through opposite paths in the interferometer pair and always arrive at the final beam splitter.

Monitoring Detector

Implementing a *monitoring detector (MD)* into a receiver's device helps to ward off thermal blinding attacks. This optical power monitor receives around 1% of the device's input. This is enough to detect any suspicious influx of heat energy typical in thermal blinding.

Delay Line

An optical *delay line (DL)* is a component which protects against Trojan horse attacks directed at the phase modulator (PM). The delay line makes it impossible for a malicious actor to detect any reflected light from the phase modulator unit before a modulated photon has been detected by Bob/the receiver.

Electronic Polarization Controller

An *electronic polarization controller (EPC)* in a receiver device functions to mitigate environmental disturbances during QKD operation (see Figure 12-3). An EPC is placed before the receiver's interferometer to compensate for the constant polarization rotations in the transmission fiber.

Fiber Length Stretcher

The path lengths of the fiber optic based interferometers in the transmitter and receiver are potentially influenced by fluctuations in temperature. To compensate for this, an electrically driven *fiber length stretcher (FS)* is placed in the receiver's interferometer.

Avalanche Photodiodes and Self-Differencing Circuits

The so-called avalanche photodiodes (APDs) are used for photon detection on Alice's/the receiver's device. A diode is simply a device which converts light into electricity. An APD is a type of diode with signal-amplifying properties. The APDs in the QKD system presented were cooled to -30° Celsius for optimal performance.

Also a part of the presented system were *self-differencing circuits (SD)* which allow the avalanche photodiodes to work effectively in the so-called Geiger-mode, without excessive levels of signal noise. In this mode a device's output pulses create "on/off" trigger events. Avalanche photodiodes operating in Geiger-mode are some of the most optimal components available today for detecting single photons.

The Externals

All of this advanced technology is housed under a rather minimalistic steel chassis as can be seen from Figure 12-4. Both the transmitter and the receiver devices measure 19"/48 cm in width and 5.25"/13.3 cm in height.

Figure 12-4. *A QKD transmitter and receiver[1]*

In Closing

After finishing this chapter, you will have learned the following:

- The major cryptographic attacks in the realm of QKD

- Which hardware components a secure QKD system consists of

In the next chapter we'll explore other current implementations of QKD, including *SwissQuantum*, *Tokyo QKD Network*, and others.

References

Dixon, A. R., Dynes, J. F., Lucamarini M. et al. Quantum key distribution with hacking countermeasures and long term field trial. 2017. `www.ncbi.nlm.nih.gov/pmc/articles/PMC5434053`

Luis Adrian Lizama-Pérez, José Mauricio López, and Eduardo De Carlos López. 2016. Quantum Key Distribution in the Presence of the Intercept-Resend with Faked States Attack. Entropy/MDPI 19.

Yusheng Zhao. 2018. Development of Quantum Key Distribution and Attacks against It. IOP Conf. Series: Journal of Physics: Conf. Series 1087.

Fabio Grazioso, Frédéric Grosshans. 2013. Photon-Number-Splitting-attack resistant Quantum Key Distribution Protocols without sifting. Physical Review A, American Physical Society.

J. Nitin, E. Anisimova, I. Khan et al. 2014. New Journal of Physics 16. Trojan-horse attacks threaten the security of practical quantum cryptography.

B. Ouchao, A. Jakimi. International Journal of Advanced Engineering, Management and Science, June 2018. Performance Evaluation of Secure Key Distribution Based on the B92 Protocol.

Yang-Yang Fei, Xiang-Dong Meng, Ming Gao, Hong Wang & Zhi Ma. 2018. Quantum man-in-the-middle attack on the calibration process of quantum key distribution. Scientific Reports volume 8.

CHAPTER 13

Implementations of QKD

Chapter 12 provided a basic overview of the hardware components in a quantum key distribution (QKD) system. We also explored the Tokyo QKD Network built to test the threat resilience of QKD. In this chapter we'll delve into larger implementations of this technology, exploring the basics of a total of five major QKD networks.

The DARPA Quantum Network

The honor of being the world's first quantum network belongs to *The DARPA Quantum Network*. Funded by the *Defense Advanced Research Projects Agency* of the US Department of Defense, this QKD system was operational between 2002 and 2007. The DARPA Quantum Network was built by *BBN Technologies* collaborating with Harvard University and the *Boston University Photonics Center (BUPC)*.

DARPA ran on unused fiber optic cable (i.e., dark fiber) beneath the streets of Boston and Cambridge, Massachusetts. The system was compatible with conventional Internet technology. It consisted of ten optical nodes, connecting Harvard University with Boston University.

© Robert Ciesla 2020
R. Ciesla, *Encryption for Organizations and Individuals*,
https://doi.org/10.1007/978-1-4842-6056-2_13

The DARPA system incorporated several QKD distribution protocols into a single protocol stack. Privacy was enhanced using *universal hashing,* in which an algorithm is chosen at random from a family of hashing algorithms. This approach contains very few probabilities for collisions and spans the mathematical domains of integers, vectors, and strings. Key sifting in DARPA was achieved by either traditional means, such as run-length encoding (RLE), or using the SARG04 protocol.

SARG04 by Scarani et al. is a more robust version of the ubiquitous BB84 protocol offering improved resistance against photon-number-splitting attacks. SARG04 works best in scenarios where attenuated laser pulses are used instead of individual photons.

Run-length encoding (RLE) is the simplest lossless form of data compression dating back to the late 1960s. Instead of including repeated sets of data, RLE stores only single sets of these duplicate repeating bits while recording the amount of times these sets are to be repeated.

Secure Communication Based on Quantum Cryptography (SECOQC)

In 2003 a grand European cryptographic project was initiated. The SECOQC was created to study the practical applications of quantum key distribution technology in the context of the Q3P protocol. The project's participants included 41 organizations from the European Union, Russia, and Switzerland. We'll next examine the findings of this rather large team of experts.

Now, there are two primary types of QKD networking approaches.

1. **Quantum channel switching.** An end-to-end quantum channel is used between transmitter and receiver (e.g., Alice and Bob).

2. **Trusted repeater.** The keys are transported over many nodes (i.e., intermediate locations) which are deemed trustworthy.

Participants in the SECOQC project focused on researching the implementation of a six-node trusted repeater network (see Figure 13-1). This came to fruition in Vienna in 2008.

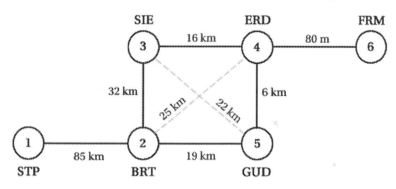

Figure 13-1. *The node layout of the SECOQC network*

The nodes were all located within Vienna, apart from *St Pölten (node 1)* which was hosted by a repeater station on a communication line from Vienna to Munich, Germany (see Table 13-1).

Table 13-1. *The SECOQC nodes*

Designation	Full Name	Designation	Full Name
STP	St Pölten	ERD	Erdberger Lände
BRT	Breitenfurterstraße	GUD	Gudrunstraße
SIE	Siemensstraße	FRM	Siemens Forum

The research group behind SECOQC identified three main components for their networking approach:

1. **The Q3P communication interface,** a quantum point-to-point protocol which provides a secure communication primitive between two adjacent nodes. It utilizes technologies such as QKD-TL and QKD-NL.

2. **QKD-transport layer (QKD-TL),** a layer responsible for linking the correct applications for quantum transmission, connection management, and network congestion control.

3. **QKD-network layer (QKD-NL),** a layer responsible for actually delivering quantum data between nodes, including data route determination.

SECOQC also highlighted some issues with implementing QKD, such as the poor rates of transmission (1 GiB per month). In addition, although the SECOQC approach was found to be completely interoperable within the framework, it's not transferable to mixed networks (e.g., consisting of both QKD and conventional TCP/IP).

Quantum Experiments at Space Scale (QUESS)

QUESS was a joint Austrian–Chinese space mission facilitated by the *Tiangong-2* space laboratory, launched in September 2016. As one part of its payload, Tiangong-2 included the tools for Space to Earth quantum key distribution. The equipment allows ground receivers, potentially separated by thousands of kilometers, to establish secure quantum channels using entangled photons. A satellite named *Micius*, named after an ancient Chinese scientist, had the honor of carrying out these tasks.

QUESS successfully demonstrated QKD between two observatories in China with a distance of over 2500 kilometers. The system also facilitated the first intercontinental secured quantum video call between China and the *Institute for Quantum Optics and Quantum Information* in Austria. The distance between these two locations spanned over 7500 kilometers. In addition, QUESS tested quantum teleportation, transmitting the states of sub-atomic particles from the satellite into a ground station in Tibet.

The main benefit of satellite-based quantum key distribution is in its greatly reduced issues with entangled particles due to scattering; both fiber optic cables and ground-based line-of-sight quantum devices suffer considerably more from this issue. However, QUESS cannot function when basking in sunlight or without direct line of sight with ground nodes.

China has the ambitious goal of creating a global QKD network using technology found in Micius satellites by 2030.

SwissQuantum

Built to test the long-term performance of a QKD system, Swiss company *ID Quantique* built the *SwissQuantum* QKD network in 2009. The system ran for two years in the Geneva metropolitan area. SwissQuantum ran between three nodes: the *University of Genova (Unige), CERN,* and *hepia (Haute Ecole du Paysage, d'Ingenierie et d'Architecture)*. Like its DARPA counterpart, SwissQuantum ran on dark fiber cables.

SwissQuantum used a three-layered approach in implementing its QKD network.

- **Quantum layer.** Consisted of point-to-point QKD links running on commercial QKD devices.

- **Key management layer.** This layer was responsible for secret key distribution across the network and between the other layers.

- **Application layer.** A layer which offers its users a graphical user interface for interacting with the QKD system.

The SwissQuantum system was monitored using three *virtual local area networks (VLAN)*. A single VLAN was assigned for each of the three layers. The system was protected by two firewalls; only ID Quantique, Unige, and hepia had access to the network.

SwissQuantum supported the similar BB84 and SARG protocols, of which the latter is more resistant against photon-splitting attacks. SARG is a better protocol for long distances and was thus chosen for use in the SwissQuantum network. The QKD key sifting was done in three steps: *error correction*, *privacy amplification*, and *authentication* of the related classical communications. The privacy amplification phase was implemented using universal hash functions.

The SwissQuantum network demonstrated that relatively complicated layered QKD systems can be a realistic and reliable solution. The CERN node resided in France, while the other two were in Switzerland (see Table 13-2).

Table 13-2. *The links and their properties in SwissQuantum*

Name	Nodes	Fiber Length	Optical Loss (dB)
SQ1	CERN-Unige	14.4 km	-4.6
SQ2	CERN-hepia	17.1 km	-5.3
SQ3	Unige-hepia	3.7 km	-2.5

Now, *optical loss* is a phenomenon which describes photon depletion over distances. In general, the longer the optical fiber cable, the more QKD-based data loss is likely to occur. A proposed solution is in *quantum repeater devices*, which would amplify the signal at specific points in the network to mitigate this issue. See Table 13-2 for some measurements of optical loss in the SwissQuantum network and how it relates to fiber length.

Not only limited to the world of audio, optical loss in fiber optic sources is denoted in *decibels (dB)*. A decibel is a relative unit of measurement used in expressing the ratio of one value to another.

Tokyo QKD Network

A collaboration between nine partners, the *Tokyo QKD Network* ran in 2010 on six nodes. In this project, gigahertz-clocked QKD systems, a QKD smartphone, a reliable commercial QKD product, and an entanglement QKD system were to be tested. For one, secure TV conferencing was achieved. Such a tested conferencing implementation incorporated an automatic communications rerouting system should eavesdropping be detected (see Figure 13-2).

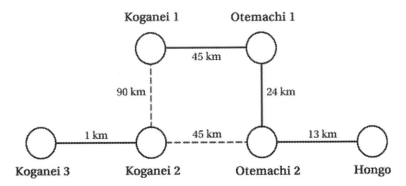

Figure 13-2. *The six-node Tokyo QKD Network configuration. Secure video communication was demonstrated between Koganei and Otemachi servers. The dashed line denotes an alternate, 135 km route for these communications (i.e., through Koganei 2 to Otemachi 2)*

Much like SwissQuantum, the Tokyo QKD Network had a three-layer approach. A *quantum layer* consists of point-to-point quantum links with each link generating a secure key using any arbitrary protocol or key format. Connected QKD devices then deliver the keys onto layer two, the *key management layer*.

In this middle layer, a *key management agent (KMA)* operates as a trusted node. Each KMA receives the makings of a key and proceeds to resize and save them. The *qubit error rate (QBER)* and the key generation rate are also stored for analysis.

The top, *communication layer*, handles numerous tasks, such as secure video conferencing and key transfer to mobile devices. The video in the system is delivered at a rate of 128 kbps, which provides somewhat passable fidelity. For comparison, a 720p video stream on a typical classical network (e.g., YouTube) is usually considered optimal at between 2000 and 4000 kbps, depending on the video protocols in use.

The teams behind Tokyo QKD Network experiments concluded that while they demonstrated long-term QKD use, the focus in this field in the near future should be on system miniaturization. Eventually, all critical levels in the Japanese government are expected to utilize QKD for their confidential communications.

In Closing

After finishing this chapter, you'll have learned the basics of five recent implementations of QKD networks, specifically DARPA, SECOQC, QUESS, SwissQuantum, and the Tokyo QKD Network. See Table 13-3 for a rundown.

Table 13-3. *Recent implementations of QKD networks at a glance*

QKD Network	Nodes	Longest Node Separation (L)/Total Network Length (T)	Area(s) of Study
DARPA	10	**L:** 19 km (BU-BBN) **T:** 29 km (Harvard-BU)	Combining QKD with classical Internet technology (i.e., TCP/IP)
QUESS	3	**L:** 7500 km **T:** n/a	Satellite-based QKD using quantum entanglement and quantum teleportation over vast distances
SECOQC Vienna	6	**L:** 85 km (STP-BRT) **T:** 200 km	Trusted QKD repeater technology, Q3P-protocol development
SwissQuantum	3	**L:** 17.1 km (CERN-hepia) **T:** 35.2 km	QKD durability in continuous operation
Tokyo QKD Network	6	**L:** 135 km (Koganei 1 - Otemachi 2) **T:** 148 km	Absolutely secure video transmission even under QKD eavesdropping

In the next chapter we'll examine many other exciting technologies the very near future holds for quantum-based computing and cryptography.

References

Elliott, C. The DARPA Quantum Network. 2004. Retrieved from arXiv:quant-ph/0412029

Peev, M., Pacher, C., Alleaume, R. et al. The SECOQC quantum key distribution network in Vienna. New Journal of Physics, Volume 11, 2009.

D. Stucki, M. Legre, F. Buntschu et al. Long term performance of the SwissQuantum quantum key distribution network in a field environment. New Journal of Physics, 13 123001, 2011.

Kramer, H. QUESS (Quantum Experiments at Space Scale) / Micius. Retrieved from: https://directory.eoportal.org/web/eoportal/satellite-missions/q/quess

Sasaki, M., Fujiwara M., Ishizuka H. et al. Field test of quantum key distribution in the Tokyo QKD Network. 2011. Retrieved from https://arxiv.org/abs/1103.3566

CHAPTER 14

Post-Quantum Cryptography

For the last few chapters, we have kept a focus on quantum key distribution, or QKD. This maturing technology is still going to be relevant for a long time. What's going to come with it is known as *post-quantum cryptography*, which will be the main topic for this chapter. We'll explore an overview of this topic, going through the basics of the most relevant approaches to encryption schemes in the post-quantum realm.

Post-Quantum Cryptography

To clarify, *post-quantum cryptography (PQC)* is a field of science in which new quantum-resistant (mostly) public-key algorithmic solutions are researched for a full variety of devices and scenarios. *Quantum cryptography*, on the other hand, often refers to the use of quantum key distribution (QKD) alongside contemporary encryption techniques, as explained previously in the book.

Now, many classical cryptographic algorithms rely either on integer factorization (e.g., RSA) or discrete logarithms (e.g., ElGamal). While offering robust security within the current computing paradigm, the near future may not be as bright for these approaches. Algorithms hazardous to contemporary encryption schemes, like *Shor's algorithm*, have been

© Robert Ciesla 2020
R. Ciesla, *Encryption for Organizations and Individuals*,
https://doi.org/10.1007/978-1-4842-6056-2_14

discovered after all. As powerful quantum computers are emerging, some effective defensive measures need to be implemented. The first line of defense is to simply increase key sizes used in contemporary encryption algorithms from, say, 128 to 256 bits (and beyond). What follows is the transition to full-scale encryption which is intrinsically quantum-resistant. Again, cryptographic schemes in this new era are referred to as *post-quantum algorithms*.

One of the biggest challenges in the near future comes in the form of integrating quantum resistance into existing devices. The potential solution of add-on hardware cryptoprocessors is in development by big business, including Microsoft and Google.

Many of today's hashing functions are largely considered immune to quantum-based hacking. However, a technique known as *Grover's algorithm* is potentially able to defeat some of these hash functions. When computing this algorithm, one is basically testing every input value simultaneously to see which is the correct one, taking advantage of quantum superposition in doing so.

Most proposed PQC protocols use an asymmetric approach. There are several major implementations of PQC being currently researched. We'll explore some of them next.

Hash-Based Cryptography

Cryptographic primitives based on the security of hash functions are generically known as *hash-based cryptography*. This variety of cryptography is currently limited to digital signature schemes. The US National Institute of Standards and Technology (NIST) announced in 2019 its intention to publish standards for stateful hash-based cryptography based on *Leighton-Micali Signatures (LMS)* and *eXtended Merkle Signature Scheme (XMSS)*. We will look at both of these schemes soon.

A *state* in the context of hashing schemes refers to recorded information, often an input password that is not to be reused. *Stateless* signature schemes do not request information/passwords after each signature is calculated.

- **Merkle signature scheme (MSS).** Although this approach dates back to the late 1970s, it's still considered to be both computationally fast and resistant to quantum computers. The Merkle scheme can be used to sign an arbitrary number of messages (to the power of two) using one public key. Merkle trees are created by repeatedly hashing pairs of nodes until there is only one hash left, which is known as the *Merkle Root* (see Figure 14-1).

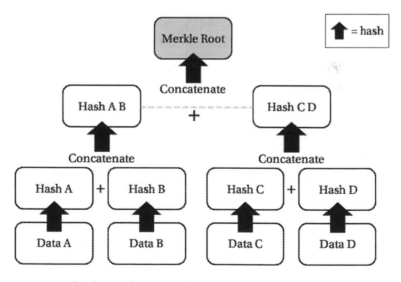

Figure 14-1. *The basic layout of a Merkle tree. Concatenation in this context refers to the process of combining hex characters. By modifying information in data nodes A, B, C, or D, the above nodes are also altered, leading to a different Merkle Root*

This root node becomes a public key; it can be then used to authenticate all other nodes. Message signing aside, a number of cryptocurrencies, including *Bitcoin*, use the Merkle tree approach for its quick and efficient data verification capabilities.

- **eXtended Merkle signature scheme (XMSS, XMSS MT).** Introduced in 2011 and not surprisingly sharing a lot with the Merkel signature scheme, XMSS is a more secure version of the venerable scheme, often producing smaller signature sizes as well. *XMSS MT* is a more powerful, multitree variant of this scheme and can in theory sign an infinite number of messages; compared to XMSS, this variant typically creates signatures faster at the cost of bigger file size (Hülsing & Gazdag).

- **Leighton-Micali Signatures (LMS).** Taking the Merkle scheme and improving on it, the basic component of the full LMS scheme is a *one-time (OT) signature scheme*. It consists of OT key generation, signing, and verifying algorithms. In the full scheme, we then combine this one-time scheme as a subroutine with a Merkle tree construction to have the full stateful LMS signature scheme.

- **SPHINCS/SPHINCS+.** Introduced in 2015, *SPHINCS* is a stateless signature scheme. A minor downside to SPHINCS is in the rather large signature size of 41 kilobytes. The scheme offers robust security against quantum computers. SPHINCS+ is an update on this approach which, for one, addresses the signature size. Even the highest security implementation of SPHINCS+ results in signatures of 30 kilobytes in size; the scheme can go as low as eight kilobytes for its lowest security level (Bernstein & Hopwood et al., 2015).

Code-Based Cryptography

This branch of quantum-resistant cryptography relies on error correction codes (ECC). Most basic cryptographic functions like encryption and signing can be implemented using code theoretic concepts. From a consumer's point of view, optimized code-based cryptography can be exceptionally fast during both data encryption and decryption, making it ideal for mobile devices with limited battery life (Engelbert, Overbeck, & Schmidt, 2007).

- The asymmetric **McEliece cryptosystem** from 1978 was the first implementation of code-based approach. This scheme uses a specific error correction code, the *binary Goppa*. A Goppa code is based on modular arithmetic, in which numbers reaching a specific target value (i.e., the *modulus*) revert back to zero again. The most common real-life example of this is the twelve-hour clock. Such a device is said to use *arithmetic modulo 12*. The McEliece aside, numerous cryptographic algorithms, including RSA and AES, leverage modular arithmetic in various ways (Engelbert, Overbeck, & Schmidt, 2007).

  - As robust as the Goppa codes are, they tend to need rather large public keys. This facet of the McEliece scheme might require some further development. Other, more lightweight codes have been proposed to replace the trapdoor functions provided by the Goppa codes, but none have proven to be as resilient to cryptanalysis (Au, Eubanks-Turner, & Everson, 2013).

- The **Niederreiter cryptosystem** is a more recent take on the McEliece cryptosystem. Developed in 1986 by *Harald Niederreiter*, the approach is considered equal to its predecessor when it comes to the overall level of security. However, Niederreiter is faster than the McEliece cryptosystem when encrypting data (Kapshikar & Mahalanobis, 2020).

Multivariate Cryptography

Multivariate cryptography is a concept referring to asymmetric cryptographic primitives based on multivariate polynomials. It represents a very robust take on post-quantum cryptography. However, as most of this technology hasn't fully matured yet as of 2020, it's feasible that undiscovered attack vectors become an issue.

- Cryptologist *Jacques Patarin* presented a public-key cryptosystem called **Hidden Field Equations (HFE)** in 1996. This was perhaps the first example of a highly secure form of *multivariate cryptography* and it remains popular today. HFE is built on the difficulty of the problems of solving a system of quadratic equations. HFE is based on polynomials over finite fields of different sizes to mask the connection between private and public keys.

- **Unbalanced oil and vinegar (UOV)** is another signature scheme by Patarin based on his earlier work. UOV depends on the difficulty of distinguishing between two types of variables it uses, referred to as "oil" and "vinegar." The term unbalanced comes from this scheme implementing a differing amount of the two aforementioned variables. In order to create and receive signatures with UOV, only a minimal quadratic equation system is to be solved. This scheme is considered quantum-resistant. UOV is also highly implementable in the most basic of hardware devices as it's mostly based on multiplication and addition. The key lengths in this scheme tend to be rather large, resulting in somewhat hefty key file sizes.

- An earlier version of UOV, known as *balanced oil and vinegar*, was broken in 1998, calling for this updated version (Kipnis & Shamir, 1998).

- **Rainbow** by *Jintai Ding* and *Dieter Schmidt* is a signature scheme based on UOV. Published in 2005, it can be described as a multilayer implementation of the aforementioned approach. While being very speedy, Rainbow shares the issue of large key and signature sizes of its predecessor(s), although to a smaller degree (Ferozpuri & Gaj, 2018).

Lattice-Based Cryptography

A *lattice* is a mathematical concept in group theory referring to repeating sets of points. Lattices are coordinate vectors in an n-dimensional space (see Figure 14-2). Perhaps the best real-life example of lattices in nature comes in the form of crystals. The term *n-dimensional space* refers to a vector space with an arbitrary number of vectors.

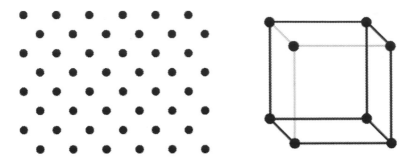

Figure 14-2. *A two-dimensional lattice (left) next to a three-dimensional lattice. The latter is 1 of 14 of the so-called Bravais lattices, representing one of their primitive types*

Lattice-based cryptography is considered extremely robust as it represents the *learning with errors (LWE)* concept. In LWE a small, controlled error is introduced to datasets to make them impossible to decrypt (at least within a reasonable time frame). This technique is a major part of machine learning. The LWE problem was introduced in 2005 by theoretical computer scientist *Oded Regev* who went on to win the 2018 *Gödel Prize.*

Decryption in LWE is done by knowing the secret error distribution which will allow the recipient to receive the actual message. Although lattice-based cryptosystems are very fast, they need large key sizes. Next, we'll review some signature schemes based on the aforementioned approach.

Lattice problems refer to a class of optimization problems which are extremely difficult to solve. These are used to create the robust cryptographic properties lattices have to offer. For one, highly collision-resistant hash functions can be built based on the difficulty of finding an approximate shortest vector in a lattice.

- **Bimodal Lattice Signature Scheme (BLISS).**
  Compared to many other approaches, this scheme
  offers smaller signature size by the use of *Huffman
  encoding*, which is a type of lossless compression.
  BLISS is also claimed to be computationally effective
  and to offer robust protection against cryptographic
  attacks (Ducas & Durmus et al., 2013).

- **Goldreich–Goldwasser–Halevi (GGH) scheme.** The
  GGH is a public-key cryptosystem which utilizes the
  closest vector problem (CVP). In this scheme both the
  public and private keys are representations of the
  same lattice. GGH offers good performance due to its
  effective leveraging of simple matrix operations.

- **GGH signature scheme.** Like the other GGH, this
  scheme uses the CVP problem for solid security, in this
  case for the purposes of digital signatures. Introduced
  in 1997, the GGH signature scheme uses an approach
  where messages need to be hashed into a mathematical
  space spanned by a lattice. The signature for a specific
  hash in this space is the closest lattice point. It's worth
  noting the most basic variant of the GGH signature
  scheme was demonstrated to be broken (Nguyen, 1999).

- **NewHope.** This extremely secure key exchange scheme
  is based on a computational problem known as *Ring
  learning with errors (RLWE)*. This provides exceptional
  performance and is simple to implement in software.
  However, it's been postulated that the standard
  learning with errors (LWE) approach might actually be
  more robust as it's been studied more thoroughly for
  threat resistance over the years (Alkim & Avanzi et. al.,
  2020).

- **NTRU** is a formerly proprietary cryptographic software consisting of two components: *NTRUencrypt*, a robust encryption solution, and *NTRUsign*, a signature scheme. NTRU was created in 1996 by mathematicians *Jeffrey Hoffstein, Jill Pipher*, and *Joseph H. Silverman*. As of 2017, NTRU has been made available in the public domain. The system is known to be both very speedy (being hailed as the fastest lattice-based system available) and quantum-resistant. A derivative of the NTRU algorithm, the *Stehle-Steinfeld*, is not considered as efficient. Another take on NTRU, *NTRU Prime*, has made it into the second round of NIST's *Post-Quantum Cryptography Standardization project*.

Homomorphic Encryption

With *homomorphic encryption (HE)*, decryption is not actually necessary to access any parts of encrypted datasets. This approach works well for health and finance sectors as at no point is decryption necessary in the traditional sense when operating on encrypted information. Critical cloud-based storage is just one example of a scenario in which (fully) homomorphic cryptography becomes highly useful. One notable feature of lattice-based cryptography is known to facilitate *fully homomorphic encryption (FHE)*, the most robust form of homomorphism, particularly well. However, homomorphic encryption can be implemented with numerous public-key algorithms such as *ElGamal* and some of its variations (Parmar, Padhar, & Patel et al., 2014).

The somewhat elderly RSA encryption method, mentioned in the previous chapters, actually represents *partially homomorphic encryption (PHE)*.

Now, there are basically three degrees to homomorphism in cryptography, each with different pros, cons, and usage scenarios. These are summarized in Table 14-1.

Table 14-1. *The three main degrees of homomorphic encryption*

Classification	Features	Potential Usage Scenarios
Partially homomorphic (PHE)	Permits either addition or multiplication on encrypted data but not both, fast computational speed	Statistical analysis
Somewhat homomorphic (SHE)	Supports more than a single type of operation, limits total number of operations	Secure databases
Fully homomorphic (FHE)	Arbitrary computation on encrypted data, slowest rate of computation	Cloud-based storage, electronic voting, managing highly classified data

Homomorphic Algorithms

There are a number of algorithms developed specifically for homomorphism. We'll review some of them next.

- **Paillier cryptosystem algorithm.** Devised by *Pascal Paillier* in 1999, this scheme is described as an *additive homomorphic cryptosystem*. The Paillier is considered particularly suitable for the purposes of electronic voting.

- **Gentry-Halevi (GH) encryption scheme**. In 2009 *Craig Gentry* described a plausible construction for a fully homomorphic encryption scheme using lattices. This was the first lattice-based software implementation of its kind. This technique was enhanced with the input of computer scientist *Shai Halevi*. The GH encryption scheme was made public in 2010.

- **The GSW cryptosystem.** Created by *Craig Gentry, Amit Sahai*, and *Brent Waters* in 2013, the GSW represents fully homomorphic encryption (FHE) implemented with a learning with errors (LWE) approach. In GSW the often computationally heavy homomorphic addition and multiplication operations are instead executed with simpler matrix addition and multiplication. Interestingly, while many other schemes require a user's "evaluation key" to be obtained, the GSW scheme has no such key (an evaluation key consists of a chain of encrypted secret keys). Homomorphic operations can be therefore executed without knowing any parts of the public key, some minor parameters notwithstanding (Gentry, Sahai, & Waters, 2013).

- The GSW cryptosystem has also been described as rather ubiquitous as it's seen much use in homomorphic signature schemes as well (Robshaw & Katz, 2016).

Bootstrapping in the context of cryptography refers to the process of minimizing "noise" a fully homomorphic encryption scheme invariably generates. Although necessary under many schemes, bootstrapping is a computationally costly procedure. Ways of mitigating its impact on computational resources include noise reduction to reduce the frequency of bootstrapping, and ditching the technique altogether, as suggested by Brakerski and Vaikuntanathan in their 2011 paper "Fully Homomorphic Encryption without Bootstrapping."

Video Gaming for Homomorphism

With the rise of 3D gaming and the associated hardware development, since the 2000s manufacturers like AMD and Nvidia have been churning out rather powerful video cards. The computing power in a *graphics processing unit (GPU)* usually used for generating dazzling vistas and scenes of simulated murder can be leveraged to provide other tasks as well.

In a 2012, a research project by Wang, Hu, and Chen et al. created a scenario in which GPU-based acceleration was applied to the fully homomorphic Gentry–Halevi scheme. It was demonstrated that using a video card to aid in computation resulted in speedup factors of 7.68 for encryption, 7.4 for decryption, and 6.59 for recryption. The experiment utilized an Nvidia Tesla C2050 from 2011, which by today's standards is only a modestly powerful card. Clustered modern GPUs offer processing capabilities greater than an order of magnitude (or several) compared to their earlier brethren.

The Tesla range of GPUs was a part of Nvidia's *general-purpose graphics processing units (GPGPU)*, which were designed with computation, not gaming, in mind. In 2020 Nvidia retired the Tesla's as the much more powerful Ampere A100 cards took their place. However, most higher-end gaming cards of recent years can be used for purely computational purposes as well.

Homomorphism for Coders

Several *application programming interfaces (APIs)* have emerged over the past few years. The two best known are the proprietary *CUDA (Compute Unified Device Architecture)* by Nvidia and the open source *OpenCL (Open Computing Language)*. The latter was introduced by Apple in 2009 but is currently being developed by Khronos Group.

In 2015 *Wei Dai* and *Berk Sunar* presented *CUDA Homomorphic Encryption Library (cuHE)*, a free programming library which takes full advantage of current-generation Nvidia GPUs in a cryptographic context. For homomorphic sorting operations alone, cuHE offers a speedup between 12 and 41 times (Dai & Sunar, 2016).

Standardizing PQC

As you probably know by now, encryption in its many forms is firmly embedded in our world, from mobile devices to government databases. A new generation of cryptographic technology must be therefore very thoroughly evaluated before widespread implementation.

The US *National Institute of Standards and Technology (NIST)* launched an initiative in 2016 to establish standards for post-quantum encryption. As of 2020, a number of proposed PQC protocols are being evaluated for use by the US government; over half of the initial 69 proposals have already been rejected.

In addition, the *Open Quantum Safe (OQS) project* aims to develop quantum-resistant cryptography, integrating current PQC schemes into a single open source programming library called *liboqs*. As of 2020, liboqs includes key exchange algorithms like NewHope and NTRU.

Zero-Knowledge Proof in PQC

A *zero-knowledge proof (ZKP)* is a technique or protocol in which a party can prove to another party that they know a secret value without disclosing any additional information. This guards the password/key from being put out there. ZKP is a crucial component in blockchains (e.g., digital currencies), online banking, ID schemes, and numerous other verification methods. Zero-knowledge protocols work for any variety of multiparty computation.

Now, there are basically three core qualities to ZKP.

- **Completeness.** If a statement is true, the verifier should be completely convinced.

- **Soundness.** A malicious prover should not be able to convince the verifier if the statement is false (a small probability aside).

- **Zero-knowledge.** A malicious verifier learns nothing except that the statement is true.

Protocols implementing zero-knowledge proofs of knowledge require input from the verifying party. This input is usually provided in the form of a set of challenges/questions. These responses will convince the verifier if, and only if, a statement is true. Zero-knowledge proofs were first formulated by *Shafi Goldwasser*, *Silvio Micali*, and *Charles Rackoff* in their 1989 paper "The Knowledge Complexity of Interactive Proof-Systems."

There is even a type of zero-knowledge proofs in which no interaction is necessary between the two parties; there are known as *non-interactive zero-knowledge proofs (NIZK)*. Back in 1988 Blum et al. introduced the idea that a small random string of bits shared by the prover and the verifier guarantees computational zero-knowledge without any interaction between the parties (Blum, Feldman, & Micali, 1988).

Commitment Schemes

Cryptographic primitives known as *commitment schemes* are often used in tandem with the approach of zero-knowledge proofs. You can think of a commitment scheme as firmly locked safe which is shipped off to the receiver. It can only be opened if/when the sender gives the combination to the receiver. Once locked, the message cannot be altered even by the sender.

Commitment scheme operation takes place in two phases. First, in the *commit phase* values are chosen. In the following *reveal phase*, the value is both revealed and verified. Perhaps the most classic example of a commitment scheme is known as *coin flipping by telephone*. For this we'll ask our old friends Alice and Bob to demonstrate.

1. Alice commits to a random bit b_A ("flips a coin") and sends the resulting commitment C to Bob. Think of C as being a securely locked safe. Alice can't change the information in this safe/commitment after sealing it and shipping it off.

2. Bob chooses a random bit b_B and sends it to Alice.

3. Alice opens the safe C to let Bob see A. Both parties compute the result using a XOR operator as follows: $b=b_A \oplus b_B$.

If either Alice or Bob is honest and chooses an actually random bit (one or zero, "heads" or "tails"), then the result will also be random regardless of what the other party picked. Coin flipping by telephone guarantees to Bob that Alice will pick her sequence of bits at random. Also, this technique convinces Alice that Bob will remain unaware of the sequence of bits he flipped to her.

In Closing

After finishing this chapter, you will have learned the following:

- What is meant by post-quantum cryptography (PQC)

- Which main algorithmic approaches for PQC are in development as of 2020

- The features and varieties of homomorphic encryption

- What zero-knowledge proof (ZKP) and commitment schemes mean

Now, after finishing this book, you hopefully have a better understanding of how contemporary encryption works while also having new tools to absorb more information on this topic in the future. You also have a basic grasp on some of the fascinating phenomena found in quantum mechanics and how these are applied in cryptography.

Stay current, stay encrypted. Keep a thirsty mind.

References

Johannes Buchmann, Erik Dahmen, and Andreas Hulsing. XMSS – A Practical Forward Secure Signature Scheme based on Minimal Security Assumptions. 2011. Retrieved from: https://eprint.iacr.org/2011/484.pdf

Andreas Hülsing, Stefan-Lukas Gazdag, Denis Butin, and Johannes Buchmann. Hash-based Signatures: An Outline for a New Standard.

Léo Ducas, Alain Durmus, Tancrède Lepoint, and Vadim Lyubashevsky. Lattice Signatures and Bimodal Gaussians. 2013.

Daniel J. Bernstein, Daira Hopwood, Andreas Hülsing, Tanja Lange et al. SPHINCS: practical stateless hash-based signatures. Eurocrypt 2015. Retrieved from: https://eprint.iacr.org/2014/795.pdf

P. Q. Nguyen. Cryptanalysis of the Goldreich-Goldwasser-Halevi cryptosystem from Crypto '97. In Proc. of Crypto '99, volume 1666 of LNCS. IACR, Springer-Verlag, 1999.

Kipnis A., Shamir A. (1998) Cryptanalysis of the oil and vinegar signature scheme. In: Krawczyk H. (eds) Advances in Cryptology — CRYPTO '98. CRYPTO 1998. Lecture Notes in Computer Science, vol 1462. Springer, Berlin, Heidelberg

Engelbert, Overbeck, & Schmidt. A Summary of McEliece-Type Cryptosystems and their Security. Journal of Mathematical Cryptology Volume 1, Issue 2, 2007.

Kapshikar, Mahalanobis. 2020. A Quantum-Secure Niederreiter Cryptosystem using Quasi-Cyclic Codes (v2). (ICETE 2018) - Volume 2 SECRYPT.

Au, Eubanks-Turner, & Everson. 2013. The McEliece Cryptosystem.

A. Ferozpuri and K. Gaj, "High-speed FPGA Implementation of the NIST Round 1 Rainbow Signature Scheme," *2018 International Conference on ReConFigurable Computing and FPGAs (ReConFig)*, Cancun, Mexico, 2018. doi: 10.1109/RECONFIG.2018.8641734.

Erdem Alkim, Roberto Avanzi, Joppe Bos et. al. 2020. NewHope. Algorithm Specifications and Supporting Documentation.

Gentry, Sahai and Waters. 2013. Homomorphic Encryption from Learning with Errors: Conceptually-Simpler, Asymptotically-Faster, Attribute Based.

Robshaw & Katz. Advances in Cryptology – CRYPTO 2016. Springer. ISBN 978-3-662-53008-5.

Parmar, Padhar, & Patel et. al. Survey of Various Homomorphic Encryption algorithms and Schemes. International Journal of Computer Applications (0975 – 8887),Volume 91 – No.8, 2014.

Wang, Hu, & Chen et. al. Accelerating fully homomorphic encryption using GPU. 2012 IEEE Conference on High Performance Extreme Computing.

Dai W., Sunar B. (2016) cuHE: A Homomorphic Encryption Accelerator Library. In: Pasalic E., Knudsen L. (eds) Cryptography and Information Security in the Balkans. BalkanCryptSec 2015. Lecture Notes in Computer Science, vol 9540. Springer, Cham.

Blum, Feldman, & Micali. 1988. Non-interactive zero-knowledge and its applications. In *Proceedings of the twentieth annual ACM symposium on Theory of computing* (*STOC '88*). Association for Computing Machinery, New York, NY, USA, 103–112. DOI: https://doi.org/10.1145/62212.62222

Index

A

Active Directory (AS), 43
Adiabatic Quantum
    Computer (AQC), 224, 225
Advanced Encryption
    Standard (AES), 24, 25, 104
  block sizes/key lengths, 33
  column-major order, 34, 35
  decryption, 41
  implementation, 32
  key expansion, 37
  row-major order, 34, 35
  SPN, 34
  stages
      add round key, 40
      bitwise shift operator, 39, 40
      MixColumns, 40
      subBytes, 38
  symmetric encryption
      system, 32
  XOR, 37
Advanced Format (AF), 54
AES New Instructions (AES-NI), 32
Albert Einstein's theory, 189–191
American National Standards
    Institute (ANSI), 23
Apple File System (APFS), 56

Application programming
    interfaces (APIs), 270
Application-specific integrated
    circuits (ASIC), 241
Archaic black holes, 193
Arrays, 25, 26
Avalanche photodiodes (APDs), 244

B

Basic Euclidean algorithm, 16
Basic Input/Output
    System (BIOS), 127
BB84
  Heisenberg's uncertainty
      principle, 228
  key sifting, 229
  no-cloning theorem, 230
  oscillations patterns, 229
  plus sign, 230
  polarization of photons, 228
Beam splitters (BS), 242
BestCrypt Container
    Encryption, 66
Bimodal Lattice Signature Scheme
    (BLISS), 265
Binary to hexadecimal
    conversion, 29, 30

© Robert Ciesla 2020
R. Ciesla, *Encryption for Organizations and Individuals*,
https://doi.org/10.1007/978-1-4842-6056-2

Printed in the United States
By Bookmasters